Southern Race Progress

Southern Race Progress

THE WAVERING COLOR LINE

Thomas J. Woofter

Introduction by Jonathan Daniels

Public Affairs Press, Washington, D. C.

TO MY WIFE ETHEL

Introduction

Apparently almost everybody has come in late to the discussion of the segregation problem in the South. Sometimes in the South today it is treated like something that fell off the moon or was dropped almost as fortuitously by a fumbling Supreme Court. And in the North the impression is sometimes given that the South itself is one furious posse pursuing every colored man who asserts his rights.

In this great question which more than any other seems today to stir men in this country and the world, all of us in the United States need to know with much more precision just what the problem is and how we reached it. Information as a basis for such understanding is being provided. Vann Woodward swept away many masks in his documented story of Jim Crow and the strange notions about the segregation which has surrounded him. But no book I know provides such an understandable personal approach to the segregation story in the lifetime of living men as this charming and challenging work by Dr. Thomas J. Woofter.

What he has written is in a real sense the autobiography of the Southerner who, long before the Supreme Court, was concerned about the tragic lapses which so often and so long segregation shielded. It is, however, the autobiography also of a Southerner named after Stonewall Jackson who has always loved the South in which he labored as a good deal more than merely a scientific sociologist to understand and aid the underpeople.

Of course, not all Southerners have shared Dr. Woofter's working faith. Many will not agree with the ideas he expounds in this book today. But genteel Southerners (there does not seem to be a more precise word than "genteel") will recognize Dr. Woofter as a gentleman who understands his region and its problems much better than those who most loudly give the impression that only Kluxers can understand the South. Dr. Woofter does not need to scream his helpful understanding based upon fifty years of creative labor in the fields about which he writes. He has, indeed, written a very quiet book but a vivid one richer in native anecdotes and homely images than in statistics. It helped me understand better this troubled South in which I live. I can think of few other books

v

so deserving of a place on the shelf of required reading for those
who would understand in depth the debate which sometimes now
seems to be restricted in participation to the extremists—the defi-
ant, the vindictive, the headlong and the stubborn.

Dr. Woofter has written a book for America, but in it he has
drawn the portrait of a Southerner—of many Southerners—who
had this problem on their hearts long before any jurists put it into
a decision of the Supreme Court. Maybe, as is said, that decision
threw the fat into the fire. The heat is high. Here is also illumina-
tion.

JONATHAN DANIELS
Raleigh, North Carolina

Preface

As these pages are being written, the press is full of reports of lawsuits, controversies, and violent emotional upheavals concerning the desegregation of schools and busses. The South is crawling with newsmen seeking the sensational. At such a time it might seem strange to attempt a book whose theme is racial cooperation for regional progress. It is difficult to separate temporary storms from persisting underlying currents. The public seems more avid for heat than light on the subject—nor is the task easier when it is undertaken in the turmoil of a national political campaign with its emphasis on blind partisanship. But, while this book does consider the status quo—i.e., the fix we are in—its chief concern is to get back of the situation of the moment to take a longer view of why we are what we are and what hope there is for racial harmony.

It does appear to me, and to others who are wiser than I, that it is a good time to balance the total liabilities and assets of race relations, rather than to become obsessed with one aspect to the neglect of all others. Accordingly I review my fifty years of close contact with and observation of issues and movements in race relations and write about the people and events which, in retrospect, impress me as having been significant in shaping the present and likely to influence the future.

The observations recorded are the result of a working association with influential people, research, and active participation in organizations whose purpose has been the improvement of race relations.

I have indeed been fortunate in working with people who have dedicated much of their lives to making things move in the South—prominent people, as well as laborers in the vineyard whose influence has been unassuming but powerful. In spite of extensive reading, I am convinced that I have learned more from these people than from books. The names of those who influenced me most appear in the appropriate places in the following pages, with references to their major contributions. These sketches are all too short but it would require a large volume to catalog their full achievements.

I have also been privileged to participate in some organizations influential in promoting Southern progress: the Phelps-Stokes

Fund in its activities to advance education; the Commission on Interracial Cooperation in its efforts to create a healthy climate of Southern opinion; the University of North Carolina in its programs of stimulating research in and about the region; the Works Progress and Farm Security Administrations in their works to ameliorate the lot of the least fortunate; the Federal Security Agency (now the Department of Health Education and Welfare) in its social security activities which have underpinned the security of the Negro—not as a Negro but as a citizen—and in its assistance to the states in strengthening health and education. So I speak not from an ivory tower exclusively.

My own research, previously published in books and special reports, ranged over a number of aspects of Southern life: It included an extended period of study of cotton plantation sharecropping and the shifts of population from farm to city, and from South to North, resulting from dissatisfaction with the meager rewards of agriculture. It touched on the relation of the "Negro problem" to the problems which confront other minority groups. It covered the living and working conditions of city Negroes, both South and North. It explored the situation in Negro health and population increase. It included the changes in the status of the Negro in the armed forces and at the ballot box. It traced the need of the Negro for greater financial security. The major part was concerned with the drive for better education and the strenuous but unsuccessful efforts of public officials to equalize educational opportunity, together with the valuable assistance which they received from organizations and foundations. It considered the extent to which Southern progress and Negro progress are mutually dependent.

But there are powerful influences which mold society but which are impossible to measure and count statistically—the traditions, beliefs, and customs of the folk. These also I have endeavored to take into account.

To summarize all this in a short volume proved an exacting task. Some experts in the field may, therefore, feel that this is a superficial book since it covers a number of topics without going into great detail about any. On the other hand those who have a special cause to plead may feel that it is not sufficiently dramatic, since its primary purpose is to record and explain rather than to praise or blame.

However, in the process of reviewing my studies, friendships, and practical experiences, certain convictions about the region have been strengthened and sharpened:

1. As the Negro progresses the South progresses, and vice versa. Their fortunes are inextricably intertwined.

2. A mutually acceptable basis for cooperation is essential to progress. Fortunately the area of cooperation is already wide, and, though it may be temporarily obscured by controversy, it is enduring.

3. If left to its own devices the South will progress but slowly in the development of the Negro; hence the value of an occasional application of the needle of criticism to puncture complacency.

4. In this situation, the average American needs to be less concerned with whether this or that action conforms to Supreme Court rulings and more concerned with whether it squares with the principles of the Supreme Ruler of the Universe.

My own work and memories have, of course, been heavily supplemented by the work of many others, too numerous to list completely here. Since I have omitted footnotes, I am happy to acknowledge my debt gratefully to the following authorities who have directly contributed material or advice on certain of the topics covered: R. P. Brooks, whose work was helpful on the plantation and the early days of the University of Georgia; Rupert B. Vance, whose detailed study of the South was drawn on, especially in relation to agriculture and the antics of demagogs; R. W. Hudgens, whose practical knowledge of sharecropping was helpful; R. C. Weaver, whose authoritative work on housing and labor was valuable; Ida C. Merriam, Ellen Winston and Thomas G. Hutton for discerning suggestions on social security and public assistance; Ambrose Caliver and J. Curtis Dixon for their practical views on education, and Harry S. Ashmore's project on recent trends in education; J. C. Evans for material on the Negro in the armed forces; Howard Odum for background material on racial beliefs and rumors; C. Vann Woodward and Jonathan Daniels for historical material on segregation and politics; and Guy B. Johnson and George S. Mitchell for their intimate and practical knowledge of the cooperative movements.

I have also had general advice and encouragement from numerous friends who have read parts of the manuscript: Lowell Mellett, Nelson and Martha Sykes, James W. Ivy, P. R. Luney, Eleanor E. A. Herring, Elda S. Bardsley, James E. White, Julie O. Kerlin, and above all my wife, Ethel M. Woofter, who has suffered with me in the effort to get ideas to march in order.

I extend especial thanks to Edwin Gunberg and Sydney D. Frissell for editorial suggestions; and to Sadie Plummer and Jessie Alverson for assistance in preparing the manuscript for publication.

THOMAS J. WOOFTER

Washington, D. C.

Contents

CHAPTER 1

Roots in the Past

This is the story of some of the most tragic and heroic events in American history primarily as I have observed them first hand. It deals with the efforts of the Southern people as they have groped their way from a slave culture to modern democratic institutions, sometimes sympathetically aided and sometimes chivvied and bullied by men of other regions. It tells of the struggle of the Negro against heavy odds to rise from complete dependency to the status of self-reliant citizen. It is a record of remarkable progress, especially rapid since World War II. Some of the events are unbelievable, some are greatly encouraging, some are best forgotten. But they did happen and I have tried to set them down accurately, with the minimum of moralizing and not too much concern as to who may be offended.

Most of the events happened during my lifetime—since 1893. Many of them happened to me. They are, therefore, related partially as autobiography. Others have come to my attention as the result of many opportunities for firsthand study of race relations. Since it is well-nigh impossible to analyze so controversial a subject as race relations objectively and without bias, I have adopted the autobiographical approach to put the reader on guard as to my biases. These biases, I must quickly point out, are of the Deep South, modified by extensive Northern exposure.

All of us—white and colored, North and South—interpret race through the film of our environment and experience. While the experience of each individual is intimately personal and in a sense unique, I am sure that at least some readers have had experiences similar in some degree to mine while many others have led quite different lives. The fact that different people see race through partially different films of experience makes it impossible to generalize about the Southern attitude, the Northern attitude or the Negro attitude. The best thing we can do, it seems to me, is take a good hardheaded look at our family, our education and community experiences; if we do this honestly, objectively, we are bound to learn a good bit about what made us what we are and why we behave as we do.

It is useful to take stock of the immediate past for that is the fabric of which the present is fashioned and because even now in the middle of the twentieth century survivals of attitudes and customs of the late 1800's still exist in certain areas and among certain elements of the American people.

Before 1900 there were two films before me which all but hid the realities of race. One was the immaturity of childhood, when impressions are naturally rosy, and the other the shelter of a serene and, for that place and time, a fairly liberal Southern family.

I was born in Macon, Georgia, less than 30 years after the realist Sherman at the head of a destroying army blazed his way to fame through that somnolent small city. I did not remain long enough to accumulate even childhood memories about the place. Several years after my birth my father moved on from a professorship at Mercer University in Macon to the faculty of Georgia Normal and Industrial School in Milledgeville. Return visits to my mother's family, however, gave me memories of my grandfather, a chipper gentleman, who hobbled about on legs of unequal length, a good bit of bone having been removed from one by crude surgery on the Antietam battlefield. There was never any sign of bitterness or word of complaint from him as to the physical handicap or wrecked fortune which befell him as direct results of the Civil War. But he did comment from time to time on the unpalatability of "coffee" made from ground persimmon seeds and the inadequacy of a handful of cracked corn to sustain a day's march.

I learned also of my great-great-grandfather, Joseph Henry Lumpkin, one of the first Chief Justices of the Georgia Supreme Court, who was noted, among other things, for having eight sons and son-in-law in the Confederate Army. My father contributed the knowledge that on his side of the family I was distantly related to Stonewall Jackson, whose name both father and I bore. Naturally, Stonewall was to me Caesar, Napoleon and George Washington all in one. It was much later that I learned something else about Stonewall which made me equally proud. When he was on the faculty of Virginia Military Institute one of his pet projects was teaching a Negro Sunday School class. A Negro pastor of the church in which he taught told me of a letter that Jackson wrote from the front to this friend, Colonel Preston, expressing deep regret that he would not be in Lexington on

Christmas to play his usual part as Santa for his little colored pupils and begging the Colonel to see to the matter for him.

On the other hand I must confess that a great-granduncle had the rather doubtful distinction of helping to negotiate the agreement which diddled the Cherokee Indians out of their homelands in North Georgia. Another ancestor, of mine, I may as well point out, codified the slave laws of Georgia.

These impressions of the influence of my ancestors in shaping my attitudes would not be complete without mention of their zeal for religion which has long been a characteristic Southern trait. My granduncle was a Methodist bishop and an uncle forsook a budding law practice of some promise to heed the call to go as a missionary to the Koreans. An aunt married a missionary to China who was entrusted by T. V. Soong with the task of bringing his daughter (now Madame Chiang Kai-shek) to this country to enter school. Since my aunt and uncle were out of the country all during my young manhood, their piety did not infect me as much as it should have but it did instill a certain admiration for sacrifice.

A discomforting twist to this admiration came later when I learned that while they were carrying the benefits of Christianity and Democracy to the "heathen", a band of Catholics from a Jesuit order in France had come to my birthplace, Macon, to found a much needed Negro parochial school, calling themselves missionaries to the Georgians. It was a shock to realize that any Georgian, colored or white, would require the ministrations of a foreign mission, but this was only one of scores of such enterprises scattered through the South.

In the 1890's practically everyone beyond the age of thirty had tasted the bitter dregs of defeat in battle or of military rule by the victor. In a few short years the South had descended from the highest rank in per capita wealth to the lowest. I suppose that if I had been mature enough to react consciously to the events which were shaping my future I would have said that the South, both white and colored, was in a state of surgical shock from the removal of the cancer of slavery. Nor had the convalescence been helped by the excesses of the reconstruction government on the one hand or the violent reaction of the white people exercised through the Ku Klux on the other. However, even before I became aware of my environment the reconstruction governments were gone (but hardly forgotten) and the organized violence of the Ku Klux was discredited (temporarily) as a means of settling anything. The South, with no further interference and with little outside help, had been left to grope its way into an uncertain future.

As W. E. B. DuBois, the brilliant Negro author, stated: "No such curious and reckless experiment in emancipation has been undertaken in modern times. Certainly it would not have been unnatural to suspect that under these circumstances the Negroes would become a mass of poverty stricken vagabonds and criminals for many generations to come and yet this has been far from the case"

Born in Mississippi, my mother was of the Deep South. Her ancestors included few large slaveholders; most were professional men—ministers, doctors, and lawyers—who were relatively tolerant, moderate Southerners. She was the oldest of eight children and had much responsibility for the younger ones, which probably helped her to cultivate a realistic attitude toward human frailty. Neither from her nor from any of my other Southern relatives do I recall ever hearing any remarks indicating prejudice or intolerance toward Negroes.

My father was farm bred; he grew up in that part of North-western Virginia which is now West Virginia. This section of substantial small farmers had traditions quite different from those of the Virginia Tidewater area. The situation is summed up in the statement that it was poorer and consequently more demo-cratical. My father's family had been Southern sympathizers dur-ing the war. There were few Negroes in his community and his early ideas on race were tolerant but based on theory rather than experience. He was inclined to take a realistic view both as to the short-comings of the South and of the Negro. He was more in-terested in remedies than in causes and keenly conscious of the difficulty of achieving progress in the atmosphere of his time.

In 1889 he was invited to come to West Point, Mississippi, to organize its infant public school system. From that time on, his passion was for development of public education in the South; he worked energetically at it throughout his active career in the capacity of training teachers and service on the Georgia State Board of Education. To him a child was a child, no matter what his color, and education was the main ingredient in his prescrip-tion for the development of human resources.

As I look back at my early contacts and environment, I see

that I was fortunate not to be taught prejudice at an early age. A review of my early experiences convinces me that my friends among the psychologists are right in asserting that race prejudice is not inborn and instinctive but is something which we acquire from experience as life brings it to us. Later I was to read testimony of the truth of this fact from the other side of the color line. In Booker T. Washington's *Up From Slavery* he tells of his early, uninhibited friendship with a white companion which cooled and became distant only after his friend returned from a sojourn away from home.

My stay in Milledgeville before I was ten embraced the years when memories are blurred by childhood impressions. Later efforts to recapture their high lights are usually uncertain because of the difficulty of knowing what is actually remembered from first hand experience and what has been learned from elders.

Milledgeville was a small town—a very small town—near the exact center of the Black Belt of Georgia where all the small towns derived their income from sales and services to surrounding cotton plantations. In good crop years the bales overflowed the warehouse space and were stored in the streets, making an excellent romping ground for small boys' games. The merchants derived some supplemental income from two schools and the state mental hospital and penitentiary. Industrial activity was limited to a small brickyard, one or two sawmills, and a practically defunct tanyard for finishing hides. Rapid transport was provided by high-stepping horses or bicycles. There were some street lights —the kind that were operated by an arc between two pencils of carbon. Some houses, those of the wealthy, had telephones but most messages were written and delivered personally.

To my youthful mind, unaware of current events, time seemed to stand still except for the succession of the seasons when shoe and stocking time was followed by barefoot time, when Fishing Creek warmed up enough for swimming, when the ripening of wild plums and blackberries was followed in the fall by persimmon, walnut, and chinquapin time—only to be succeeded again by shoe and stocking weather. One of my clearest early memories was of reports of the Spanish-American War when Southerners proudly fought side by side with the Yankees and we sang "Just Break the News to Mother" and "The Old Flag Never Touched the Ground".

In those days when grown-up talk had little meaning for me,

the grown-ups were, without realizing it, discussing changes which were to be of tremendous significance in shaping the destiny of the South and the nation in the twentieth century.

The new legal doctrine of "separate but equal", cloaked with constitutionality by the Supreme Court, was popularized by the brilliant white orator Henry W. Grady. To the equally brilliant colored orator, Booker T. Washington, this doctrine was "as separate as the fingers but as united as the hand." Realistic products of their times, both of these giants were dedicated to easing tensions and bitterness between South and North and between black and white so that a sick society could become whole. Both recognized the strengths and weaknesses of the material they had to work with and made compromises with which they were not too happy.

On the plus side, the seeds of industry were sprouting. Primitive water wheels were rapidly giving away to hydroelectric power. The foundations of extraordinary technical development were being laid. Duryea was still experimenting with his gasoline buggy, Edison developed his kinetoscope, Roentgen gave us X-rays, Marconi flashed his first wireless message across the Atlantic and Curie's discovery of radium was soon crowded off the front page by the first flight of the Wright Brothers. The newly founded public schools were expanding bringing this twentieth century scientific knowledge Southward.

But there were unfavorable trends also. The post-reconstruction South which had been controlled by the moderate aristocrats, who were tolerant but paternalistic in race relations, was giving way to the rule of the crackers, led by demagogs who made race hatred their chief stock in trade. The chains of disfranchisement and segregation were being forged. The plantation system which was to dominate the rural life of a rural section was becoming firmly established. The 1890's were not gay in Dixie. They were a decade of transition. The old South was in labor bringing forth the new.

To those who are impatient with or intolerant of conditions in the South today I can only say that they should have seen it at the beginning of this century. Those who attempt to measure progress from month to month or even from year to year and become discouraged I can invite to look at the long time sweep of change which is outlined in the ensuing chapters. To them I can only say that if we work long enough and persistently enough conditions change—usually for the better.

CHAPTER 2

Cotton and Culture

My high school and college days were spent in the remarkable little city of Athens, Georgia. Its claim to fame, according to the local wags, was the possession of the only double-barreled cannon in the world, the tree that owned itself and the only firehouse that was ever burned down. My own lasting impression of the people is that they were proud, dignified, and courteous. In fact, we were so courteous that we tipped our hats not only to the ladies but also to the university professors. This courtesy did not extend to the Negro Athenians, but strenuous effort was made not to be rude. In the case of Sam Harris, the Negro principal of the high school, it seemed too crude for the white people to call him "Sam" but they could not or would not call him "Mr."; he therefore became "Dr." Harris. There were many honorary doctor's degrees conferred in this way.

When we walked to school every morning we passed a group of Negro pupils on their way to their school in the opposite direction. There was often spirited competition for the occupancy of the narrow sidewalk, not especially as racial rivalry, but simply as a form of interscholastic athletics. One morning, after a large and energetic Negro girl had pushed most of us white boys off of the sidewalk, the rocks and clods began to fly. Not much damage was done because the school bells called each party away from the combat in order to be on time. In the middle of the morning the principal of the Negro school showed up at our school with the complaint that we white boys had been too rough. He was received by our principal with great courtesy and the problem was discussed dispassionately. We were given a dressing down by our principal just as if we had been in a fight with other white pupils.

Personally, I prefer to look back on Athens as the city of cotton and culture. It was the market center for Northeast Georgia and at the same time the site of the State University and the State Woman's College.

The layers of the city were all crossed by Broad Street. This thoroughfare originated in the eastern part of town across the

Oconee River from the town proper. Its first blocks were in a Negro suburban settlement where the majority of families owned their own homes. Next it traversed the cotton mill section, an area occupied entirely by the white workers in the small cotton mill. After crossing the river it was the center of a section of cotton warehouses and fertilizer and wholesale grocery merchants. The cotton compress and the "dispensary", the county licensed store for selling whiskey, were there also. On this lower end of Broad Street, crowds of countrymen, white and colored, congregated on Saturday afternoons with much loud talk and laughter. It was unusual to walk through this part of town on Saturday without hearing the bray of a homesick mule. White women would not venture here on Saturday.

Climbing the hill, the street then passed in front of the State University. It was the boundary between the campus, which was state property, and the city controlled by local police. Thus, it marked the beginning of protection for students pursued by the police; they were safe from arrest after crossing this sanctuary.

It then dipped down into a low-lying area, which was one of the principal Negro settlements in town. Here the large families spilled out of dilapidated houses on bare, treeless yards. Waste water was thrown out in back yards and open privies decorated the landscape. I soon learned that this Negro property was one of the highest paying investments in town. The houses cost little to build and practically nothing to keep in repair. The tenants were glad to get anything to keep them out of the rain so the holders of this property often netted 15% and 20% on their investment. This was a substantial source of income for one of the more sanctimonious deacons in the Baptist church who always passed the collection plate on Sunday. A few Negroes also had acquired rental property and their terms were no easier. From the central Negro section the street climbed up to cross Milledge Avenue, the fashionable residential neighborhood. After crossing Milledge, it again wandered off into the suburbs through another large settlement of Negroes many of whom were employed in the homes of white families on Milledge Avenue and neighboring streets.

Just off Broad Street there was a small Negro business section the center of which was a "skyscraper" of four stories owned by the town's wealthiest Negro, "Pink" Morton, who had been started off in life with a small donation from his former owner, had served awhile as postmaster and had built up a fairly respectable accumulation, part of which was the Morton Building. In his building was a colored pharmacy operated by a graduate pharmacist. "Pink" Morton was one of a small group of respected Negro leaders, others of whom were Professor Harris, the high school principal, and Professor Harris' brother who was a legitimate doctor by reason of a degree in medicine.

"Pink" Morton and a few other colored families lived in a white neighborhood—in fact they had been living there since before most of the white people moved in. Nobody paid any particular attention to this phenomenon and nobody thought it unusual. One of the houses was occupied by a well-respected and financially comfortable cateress who took care of all the big parties. Many of the white people could not pass her house without remembering that she had cooked their wedding cake, another by Sam McQueen, owner of the town's best barber shop.

Other Negroes who were rising above the mass were scattered through the town. These were the preachers, postmen, teachers, owners of small business establishments, and a wide variety of skilled tradesmen. The artisans were just beginning to feel the effects of white competition as white unions were not organized in Athens until about 1912. There was little contact between white people and this upper tenth who were off in a world of their own. The white Athenians may have been vaguely aware of their existence but probably never pondered their significance for the future Negro and the South.

Increasing numbers of Negroes were acquiring property in modest amounts. In 1912 Negroes held property assessed at over a quarter of a million dollars the assessment being about two thirds of the true value. The holdings were for the most part small owner occupied homes averaging slightly over $400 in assessed value.

The most frequent contacts were between white employers and the two classes which comprised two-thirds of all Negro workers, common laborers and domestic servants.

The majority of this class of Negroes were, at that time, illiterate many of them having only recently moved into town. Some, showed a remarkable native intelligence. My mother was continually keeping complicated accounts for the cook who could not read and write. The cook would borrow $5, agreeing to pay it back weekly. Having paid it off part way another emergency

would call for another loan of $5, bringing the total debt to say
$7. The process of paying off would begin again, sometimes
regularly and sometimes irregularly. It was a little difficult for
my mother to keep track of it even with a notebook but the cook
always knew from memory where she stood to the penny.

The unskilled laborers were engaged in the hot and heavy work
of the batting mills, warehouses, and fertilizer factories. They
monopolized the jobs as drivers and porters. In street and railway
maintenance gangs they swung their picks and shovels to the
tunes of Casey Jones, John Henry, or just something they made
up on the spur of the moment. Their contacts were for the most
part with middle-class rather than upper-class whites since they
were bossed by men most of whom would, if in uniform, have
made good sergeants.

By far the most frequent and the most intimate contacts were
between white women employers and their domestic servants.
Negro wages were so low that many women had to work to help
support the family. Domestic service was the only occupation open
to women aside from a few seamstresses, practical nurses and
clerks. About 300 worked in white homes and twice as many
remained in their own home and "took in washing". Just as the
men were working out a new way of life on the plantation, so
the women were working out a new way in the kitchen and not
doing a much better job. The opinions and attitudes of the
kitchen and plantation were becoming more and more dominant
in shaping race relations and attitudes.

I had occasion to examine this relationship closely not only in
my own home, but also in connection with some research at the
University. I visited all the Negro homes and questioned most of
their employers. In spite of the crudity of my style and the immaturity of my observations I think that my first-hand observations of a peculiarly Southern institution may be worth citing:

"The number of inefficient servants is increasing, because
domestic service no longer occupies the place which it did in the
estimation of the Negro. In fifty years, domestic service has been
lowered from the highest place in the Negro's estimation to the
lowest. On the plantation there were the field hands and the
domestics; the latter being picked men and women, the most intelligent Negroes on the place and, in most cases, mulattoes. However, the generation of whites which cherished domestic servants
as the most intelligent and trusted Negroes on the place and gave

them the most honored position in the big house, looking on them as trusted friends, has passed away to be replaced by a generation which does not comprehend the paternal relation which existed between master and servant before the war. Among the Negroes that generation which looked upon domestic service as a responsible and meritorious position has in its turn been replaced by a generation which is entering more and more into the commercial, industrial, and professional fields.

"The emancipation of the slaves broke down the artificial system of selecting domestic servants. Newer and more desired fields of employment were opened to the Negro, fields into which the more efficient strove to go. This set the process of selection in motion. The best, most reliable, and competent went into the professions and the skilled trades, leaving the backward and unprogressive class to serve as domestics. It is the incompetence of this backward class who come most closely in contact with the whites that gives the Southerner the idea that the Negro has made and can make little progress.

"In addition to this change in attitude towards domestic service, another social change working among the Negro takes many of the best domestics out of service, namely, the development of home life. But as the best Negro women become homemakers the quality of domestic servants declines.

"The Negroes are less and less willing to perform the duties of two servants for small families. The only common combinations are those of butler and driver, and nurse and maid. In a few instances a single servant performs the duties of cook and chambermaid, but these are becoming rare. The washing is always done by a separate servant. It therefore appears that the service rendered by the Negro servants is by no means as much as that rendered by the average Northern white servant. This fact explains to an extent the low scale of wages that prevails throughout the South for domestic service.

"By far the most interesting and peculiar feature of the servant problem in the South is the practice of hiring on the basis of sketchy reference. A few housekeepers get a sort of recommendation in the following manner: they obtain from the applicant the name of a recent employer, ask a few questions as to honesty and regularity, and usually hire the servant without reference to her knowledge of cooking and trust to chance for the rest.

"In almost any other country a servant without reference would have small chance of employment. In the South, however, so great is the disinclination of Negroes to go into domestic service, that housekeepers are glad to get any Negro who will stay in the kitchen and relieve them of the heavy work which is necessary in keeping the style of houses generally built.

"Some housekeepers will, when asked about a servant, give a recommendation when in reality the servant had been unsatisfactory. This is done to keep from having a "bad name" among the Negroes, for the Negro women in their social meetings are given to comparing notes as to the desirability of work in various families. Almost any Negro in domestic service in Athens can tell which housekeepers are "finicky," or hard to please. In fact, so widely know are the methods of individual housekeepers, and so strange to the whites is the inner life of the darker half of the population, that it is believed by some that a black list is kept by the Negro lodges, and that the servants keep "tabs" in this way on their employers. Inquiry, however, failed to reveal any indication that such was the case in Athens.   ,

"With these facts in mind, it is not strange that only a few housekeepers ask for references, and of these some ask only as to the servant's honesty. The result of this method of hiring, forced upon the housekeepers by the scarcity of good servants and the inconvenience of the Southern houses, is that domestic service is thoroughly disorganized and unsatisfactory. In many cases incompetence is winked at by the housekeepers for the simple reason that they cannot afford to lose their servant at any cost.

"Another source of worry to the housekeeper is that servants quit frequently without notice and go into other avenues of employment for short times. The average Negro likes a short-time job. The pay for such odd jobs is generally a little higher per day and the employee can make enough money in this time to live for a month or so after the job runs out. This is especially true in cotton picking time. There is a great demand for cotton pickers in the belt of counties surrounding Athens and numbers of servants leave in the late summer and early fall to go to the country. For this work they are paid by the hundred pounds picked. If they prefer they may work slowly, practically taking a vacation, and still make enough to live on. If they work well, they can make enough to rest in ease for a time after they return to the city.

"Still another feature of Negro service objected to by some housekeepers, but taken philosophically by others as a result of custom, is the 'service basket' or pan. This carrying off of broken victuals, which is, in a majority of cases, stretched into the carrying off of small amounts of supplies from the pantry, is known among the servants as 'toting' and is almost universally practiced by the domestics of the South.

"One of the housekeepers said that the last servant who applied to her for a position stated that her usual wages were $10.00 per month when she toted, and $12.00 when she did not. Another housekeeper answered the questionnaire with a note that, having recently moved to Athens, she had not employed a servant. She stated that she was afraid of the cost of this item of food carried off. In her characteristic, though exaggerated, phrasing she voiced the sentiment expressed by many when she remarked, 'None employed. I found that the service basket feature in Athens is a serious matter. Have never seen a town like it. Just note the heavy laden cooks going home in the evening. If a Negro man or boy emerged from the rear of a store with a pair of cheap shoes under his coat the officers would chase him all over the country and finally send him to the chaingang. Every day the Negro women, often reinforced by the entire family, carry away from Athens homes supplies of groceries many times the value of the pair of shoes. They do it openly, boldly, in fact consider it one of the perquisites of their employment'.

"Of the 138 housekeepers reporting as to service basket, 52 reported that they did not allow the practice, 15 of these qualifying their answer by such phrase as 'Not to my knowledge.' The other 86 answered 'yes'. About half of these were not content with the simple affirmation, but answered with such phrases as 'certainly,' 'always and forever,' or 'three big ones each day.' Such answers would indicate that this is a thorn in the flesh, but one not easily removed.

"The question of honesty is closely related to the service basket in the mind of the housekeeper. The general opinion among the housekeepers seemed to be that servants are honest except where food is concerned. The Negroes themselves regard food in their employer's house as theirs and take it without feeling that they are committing a theft. Of the 40 housekeepers who did not absolutely affirm their servant's honesty, only eight actually denied it. The other qualified their answers. . . ."

This investigation had a blind spot in that it did not delve into the parallel opinions of the servants about their employers.

It would have been useless to solicit such opinions as no white questioner would have received frank answers. Had it been possible to probe the servants minds, low wages would have undoubtedly been high on the list of complaints. The average wage of cooks was $2.72 per week (worth about $7.50 in present day inflated money) and of maids still less. The housekeepers said that this amount was about doubled by the food eaten and carried home. The sudden decisions of cooks to take unannounced leave from their jobs was doubtless due as much to their being fed up with the conditions of work as it was to shiftlessness as stated by their employers. Many were too timid to state their complaints and the line of least resistance was to quit without argument.

Athens was in a way an island of peaceful race relations even though there were rough places near by. Lynchings had occurred in places less than 30 miles away. Nearby a farmer, who now rests under the largest monument in the local cemetery, was amassing a huge fortune by working his land with convict labor, which could be done in those days. Athens, however, wrinkled its aristocratic nose at these things without much comment or criticism. It was a very tolerant place.

The Ku Klux Klan never was able to get a hold here. A feeble effort was made to organize the Klan, but it was broken up in a novel way by a young local lawyer. When the Klanners fell behind in their payment of rent for their lodge hall, the lawyer asked the landlord to be allowed to collect the claim. He got a key and went up to the Klavern and found that all of the members had their robes and hoods hanging around the wall. Each robe had the name of the owner sewed in the collar. All the lawyer needed to do was to let it be known that he had copied a complete list of the members and was planning to make it public unless they paid up their rent and disbanded. So that was that.

Athens was also unique in supplying the only four-year public high school for Negroes in the State. This was accepted by the white people as a matter of course, even though neither Atlanta nor any of the smaller cities had more than a two-year high school. Our public schools enrolled 1,000 Negroes and the private schools another 700, many of whom were boarders from surrounding counties. The standards of these schools were higher than those in other Georgia cities but still far behind those for white pupils. Although the population of the city was two-fifths Negro, they received only one-fifth of the school funds.

Athens was also the location of the J. Thomas Heard University. This Negro institution operated mostly at night with a faculty of two in a ramshackle frame building. The most advanced students were not above the level of the sixth grade. At the time I could only see the ludicrous pretentiousness of calling it a university. It was not until later when the wife of the founder told me that it had been established with the hope that it would grow up to its name and became a force for the uplift of the race that I sensed that this was a groping for the stars by one who was too far down and whose arms were too short even to reach the treetops.

Athens revisited in 1956 forcefully reminded me of the change in the South. The city has more than doubled in size but the proportion of the races is about the same. Like her metropolitan contemporaries, Athens has suburbanized and both races have improved their living conditions by moving from the central area to the outskirts. Instead of alternating between residence and business occupancy, Broad Street now has residences on the outer ends and business in the middle. The shabbiest houses which were in the middle have been torn down. Near the western end a fairly new Negro public housing development, which appears similar to its white counterpart, has absorbed many of the families which were formerly crowded out of the poorer central sections. A few blocks farther a section of Negro home owners has developed.

Nearby, a new Negro high school is under construction, not so large as the million dollar plant for white pupils since the Negroes make up only about a third of the population, but equally as modern. There were also two recently built Negro elementary schools. In the past forty years, in fact, all of the schools for Negroes have been rebuilt and they are now housed far better than we white children were when I lived there. But the white schools have also been so improved that the difference in the provision for the two races is still appreciable.

Some of my friends are still able to afford domestic servants on professors' salaries but the wage is $10 and $12 a week instead of $3 and less. Supplementing the money income by toting food home is still an accepted practice and as many employers as ever are involved in the complicated financial affairs of their servants through advances to make a down payment on a home or to keep up the payments on an automobile. In other words the personal relationship is much the same, but the level of living of the Negro is higher.

CHAPTER 3

Southern Old Ivy

In 1908, I proudly enrolled in what we called the oldest State University. As a matter of fact there were three universities which shared this title: the University of Virginia, because it was conceived first by Thomas Jefferson; the University of Georgia, because it was chartered first in 1785; and the University of North Carolina, because it was opened first in 1795. Georgia's claim originated when Abraham Baldwin, a member of the Yale faculty, moved to the state soon after the close of the Revolution. As a member of the Georgia Legislature, he persuaded that body, in 1784, to donate 40,000 acres of land for a public institution of learning. In the following year he secured a charter for the University of Georgia, preceding the University of Virginia charter by more than 30 years.

Alas, however, the eyes were bigger than the pocketbook. The 40,000 acres of land were practically worthless since many other thousands of acres were being granted free to veterans of the Revolutionary War and the state did not appropriate any funds. The university could not therefore, scrape together the money to hire a faculty and enroll students for another 16 years, not until 1801. In the meantime, some of the hesitancy about getting started arose from the fact that each county in the state was represented by a trustee and whenever the board would try to select a site each member would vote for his own county until adjournment.

The preamble which Abraham Baldwin drew up for the charter of the University of Georgia was strikingly like that which Jefferson wrote later for the University of Virginia. The two men must have been in close touch, swapping ideas with each other; significantly, both also drew upon the ideals of the French philosophers of the time. Jefferson's first formulation of his philosophy came in 1777 when he wrote the "Bill for the more general diffusion of knowledge." This measure contemplated not only a state university, but also a complete public school system for Virginia. It was, of course, far too radical for the aristocrats of that time; many of them looked on Jefferson's plans in much the same way as Senator McCarthy looks on the Communism today. The wording of this bill is worth quoting since it was the inspiration of advocates of public education throughout early America:

"A Bill for the more general diffusion of knowledge, proposed by the Committee of Revisors of the Laws of Virginia, appointed by the General Assembly in the year 1776.

Section 1. Whereas it appeareth, that however certain forms of government are better calculated than others to protect individuals in the free exercise of their natural rights, and are at the same time themselves better guarded against degeneracy, yet experience hath shown, that, even under the best forms, those entrusted with power have, in time, and by slow operations, perverted it into tyranny; and it is believed that the most effectual means of preventing this would be to illuminate, as far as practicable, the minds of the people at large, and more especially to give them knowledge of those facts which history exhibiteth, that, possessed thereby of the experience of other ages and countries, they may be enabled to know ambition under all its shapes, and prompt to exert their natural powers to defeat its purposes; and whereas it is generally true that that people will be happiest whose laws are best, and are best administered, and that laws will be wisely formed, and honestly administered, in proportion as those who form and administer them are wise and honest; whence it becomes expedient for promoting the public happiness that those persons, whom nature hath endowed with genius and virtue, should be rendered by liberal education worthy to receive, and able to guard, the sacred deposit of the rights and liberties of their fellow citizens, and that they should be called to that charge without regard to wealth, birth or other accidental condition or circumstance; but the indigence of the greater number disabling them from so educating at their own expense, those of their children whom nature hath fitly formed and disposed to become useful instruments for the public, it is better that such should be sought for and educated at the common expense of all, than that the happiness of all should be confided to the weak or wicked. . . ."

Baldwin and Jefferson saw eye to eye on these principles. They probably discussed them together during the exciting days of the nation's formation. The extent of agreement between these two pioneer educators is apparent from a parallel reading of Baldwin's phrasing for the charter of the University of Georgia:

"As it is the distinguishing happiness of free governments that civil order should be the result of choice and not necessity, and the common wishes of the people become the laws of the land, their public prosperity, and even existence, very much depends upon suitably forming the minds and morals of their citizens. Where the minds of the people in general are viciously disposed and unprincipled, and their conduct disorderly, a free government will be attended by greater confusions and with evils more horrid than the wild uncultivated state of nature. It can only be happy when the public principles and opinions are properly directed, and their manners regulated. This is an influence beyond the stretch of laws and punishments, and can be claimed only by religion and education. It should therefore be among the first objects of those who wish well to the national prosperity to encourage and support the principles of religion and morality, and early to place the youth under the forming hand of society, that by instruction they may be moulded to the love of virtue and good order." The early educational philosophy of the South was opposite to that of New England. The "Old Ivy" in the South was, and still is, in State Universities established by the State to train leaders for the State. The Ivy League of New England consisted of private and church endowed universities, with public education centered on the lower grades. In fact, much of the public education of New England was aimed at religious training and the preservation of the protestant faith.

The Massachusetts "Old Satan" Act is often cited as an example. That this was a church and not a state act is plain from its language:

"It being one chief project of that old deluder, Satan, to keep men from the knowledge of the Scriptures, . . . that learning may not be buried in the grave of our fathers in the Church and Commonwealth, the Lord assisting our endeavors

"It is therefore ordered, that every township in this jurisdiction, after the Lord hath increased them to the number of fifty householders, shall then forthwith appoint one within their town to teach all such children as shall resort to him to write and read, whose wages shall be paid either by the parents or masters of such children, or by the inhabitants in general, by way of supply, as the major part of those that order the prudentials of the town shall appoint."

Both Jefferson and Baldwin envisioned a complete school system, but in the case of Georgia, money was not available until long after the charter was issued. Some academies were established which correspond roughly to the present day high schools. In the case of Virginia, Jefferson's plan was not during his lifetime implemented below the level of the State University because the conservative tradition of the early aristocrats held that elementary and high school education should be taken care of by the family or in private institutions.

During its first half century the University of Georgia went through a series of ups and downs—mostly downs—but it still managed to train a varied assortment of Senators, Supreme Court Justices, many Confederate Generals, the discoverer of ether as an anesthetic, the Vice President of the Confederacy, and a few real statesmen. When I came along there were still bullet pocks in the walls of the chapel as a reminder of the activities of Sherman's foraging parties and of the years when the university had been completely closed because all prospective students and professors were away in gray uniforms.

According to present-day scale, the University of Georgia, in 1908, was so small that it would now be considered almost insignificant. It was just reaching the enrollment level of 600 students. After my graduation I was much chagrined to learn, when I matriculated at Columbia University for advanced studies, that my Alma Mater was not accredited and that for admission of full standing as a graduate student I had to go through a probationary period. In these years there were only a handful of Southern universities from which the large graduate institutions accepted candidates for advanced degrees without a probationary period.

The course of undergraduate study was narrow and great emphasis was placed upon Latin, Greek and ancient history. I remember hearing some of the arguments between my father and the more conservative members of the faculty over whether or not a modern language should be substituted for either Latin or Greek on an elective basis. Another spirited battle between the progressive and the classical wings of the faculty raged over the introduction of a course in agriculture. Who ever heard of giving academic credit for the mastery of such a practical subject as farming! The institution had for years been accepting the federal grant for the teaching of agriculture, the mechanical arts, and military science. The only thing which had been done to make the claim to this appropriation legitimate was to go heavy on the military science and ignore the other two. Nevertheless it required

a stout heart and agile footwork on the part of Chancellor Walter
B. Hill to introduce the agriculture course with one professor a
few years before I entered. While I was still enrolled the growing
department was moved to a new building from its original quarters
in a small house, which had been built as a residence. The need
for the application of brains to the land of the state, for training
teachers of high school agriculture and the expanding corps of
extension agents soon ballooned the enrollment to the point that
the College of Agriculture was almost as large as all the rest of
the university.

What was taught might leave much to be desired, but there
could be no quarrel with the way in which it was taught. The
members of the faculty were dedicated to their work and
thoroughly grounded in their subjects. Grading was strict and
absences were meticulously checked. Once when a dance had
lasted too far into the morning for me to get home to change, I
attended the early classes in a dress suit to avoid absent marks.
They saw to it that what we learned was thoroughly learned.

Training of this kind naturally did not give us any too much
discernment. Knowledge of contemporary problems was not the
primary objective. We were supposed to absorb knowledge about
the present from the past as the butter absorbs the odor of the
cantaloupe in the ice box. The only social science offered, aside
from a few history courses, was a half-year course in elementary
economics in which the subject became truly the dismal science.
Just before my senior year R. P. Brooks, who had been doing
graduate work at Wisconsin, returned and introduced a course
called Georgia history and economics which was designed to throw
light on the contemporary scene. As I recall, I was one of three
students first to take this course. At the time, Wisconsin was
pioneering in the development of a university whose function was
to serve the State. This was about the first practical demonstration
of Jefferson's philosophy of training for political leadership and
service.

Another pioneer experiment along this line was taking place
under the leadership of Dr. E. C. Branson in the State Normal
School also located in Athens. His plan was to organize Georgia
clubs among the students; their purpose was to study the social and
economic conditions of the State and especially of the student's
own county. After a few years of promoting this idea in Athens,
Dr. Branson was called to wider service in the same capacity at the

University of North Carolina where he carried on successfully for many years.

We were all out for oratory. Every student had to belong either to the Phi Kappa or the Demosthenian Literary Society whose sole purpose in life was debating. However, we seldom debated subjects that struck too close to home. We would talk about woman suffrage, the tariff, and the regulation of railroad rates in an abstract manner but never anything about local economic or social conditions.

I don't recall that any of my courses, except the one in Georgia history and economics, ever mentioned any subject connected with race except as a cause for the Civil War. In our informal discussions, however, I did pick up from other students a good deal of Southern ideology of race. Considerably later Dr. Howard W. Odum in *Race and Rumors of Race* attempted to summarize this ideology as follows:

"1. That the Negro was a Negro and always would be that and nothing more.

"2. That, being a Negro, and different from the white man he therefore could not be expected ever to measure up to the white man's standards of character and achievement."

From this the correlaries developed that the Negro was predisposed to disease and incapable of developing mechanical aptitude.

"3. That, not being capable of full achievement and being of an inferior race, it was logical that he should be kept in an inferior place, which is 'his place.'

"4. It followed that this was a white man's country, and that therefore the white man would dominate in about whatever way he chose. Laws and resolutions only made matters worse.

"5. Political equality and equal educational opportunities, if given to the Negro, would lead to social equality and the mixture of races, which was contrary to all the major premises of the southern way of life.

"6. Furthermore, political and social equality would lead to the domination of the white South by the Negroes and their northern supporters.

"7. Discrimination and segregation, therefore, were necessary to keep the Negro in his place and protect the interests and integrity of the whites.

"8. It was assumed, from this point on, by the best of the South, that the Negro, when kept within his rightful sphere, should not be treated unkindly or unjustly.

"9. That he should be given fair trials and protected by law.

"10. That he should be paid a living wage. Since, however, his standards of living were lower, he could live on less than a white man could.

"11. That if given too much pay, he would waste the money and get out of bounds to his own harm as well as the detriment of the South.

"12. That the Negro was by nature inclined to criminal behavior, partly because of his animal nature and partly because of his irresponsibility and immorality.

"13. Moreover, the Negro was better off in the South where he was "understood" and where his best friends were.

"14. That, while as a race the Negro was inferior and generally untrustworthy, as an individual he was often honest, loyal, lovable, capable, and even talented and distinguished. Yet this was the exception.

"15. That his music, his carefree, patient disposition, his homely philosphy added interest and color and richness to the culture of the South.

"16. That recognition should be given to the Negro for having made outstanding progress in many fields since being freed from slavery.

"17. Yet the Negro in general was not capable of taking great responsibility or of assuming leadership.

"18. That no self-respecting Southerner would work under Negro supervision.

"19. That if the Notherners and reformers would let the South and the Negro alone, peaceful adjustments of the race problem would be made.

"20. That those who were inviting the Negro to discontent and trying to force his participation in industry and politics on an equal basis were fomenting race riots which would hurt both whites and Negroes and the total Nation in the long run.

"21. And that, finally, this was not a debatable issue."

Preposterous? So they may seem now but they didn't seem that way to me in 1910. Like all traditional beliefs, they were accepted quite uncritically. They were supposed to be right and not subject to debate. It cannot be said that they were the firm beliefs of all of the people all of the time but they were certainly held by some of the people most of the time and by most of the people some of the time. They were sufficiently authoritative to shape the code of conduct in race relations and rationalize its rightness. Some of this credo has lost much of its power in wide areas of the South with the passage of time but in backward areas of the Black Belt, where the thinking on race has not changed markedly for a century, they are still current and still potent.

"Uncle" Dave Barrow, the Chancellor, was the most outstanding character in the University picture. He was respected and beloved not only by the students but by the whole State. To many, in fact, the University meant "Uncle" Dave, and at times it appeared that the legislature felt it could get along without much money as long as it had "Uncle" Dave, and at times it almost did.

It was through him that I received my first opportunity to probe inquiringly into the racial situation in the South. Descended from slaveholders with morals, he had acquired a fine tolerance and genuine affection for colored people without being blinded to their weaknesses. In referring to his Negro wet nurse he used to say: "I did not have any Negro blood in me but I was surely full of Negro milk." In my senior year the Phelps-Stokes Fund offered to the University of Georgia and to the University of Virginia fellowships to be granted for the study of race. Prior to that time it had never entered my head that race was a topic worthy of serious study but Uncle Dave called me into his office, expressed some of his own deep concern for harmonious race relations and persuaded me to take the Phelps-Stokes Fellowship in its first year of operation. Not that I needed much persuasion; I think that Brooks' course on Georgia history and economics had opened my mind to reception of such new ideas.

It was at this point I became acquainted with the fiery little Welshman, Thomas Jesse Jones, then organizing the work of the Phelps-Stokes Fund, with whom I was later to work closely. As a Welshman among Englishmen he had some first-hand knowledge of the feelings of a member of a minority group. He imparted to me some of his respect for hard facts and impatience with pretense and false sentiment. His warmth of spirit and adherence to fundamental principles were later to gain for him a world wide reputation in the field of education for disadvantaged peoples.

My year under the Phelps-Stokes Fellowship was occupied with getting acquainted with the scanty literature on the situation in race relations at that time and writing a report entitled *The Negroes of Athens, Georgia*. Some of its findings were cited in the preceding chapter.

The one lasting impression which I have retained from this experience was my first taste of the feeling of isolation which came to a Southerner forty years ago who was a moderate on questions of race. Not that I was then a flaming liberal. I was simply doing something which, to the people of my home community, was unprecedented. They were all most polite and non-committal, because I was working under the sponsorship of the University, but no one showed any interest in discussing what I was doing beyond the exercise of a mild curiousity. I did sense, however, some lifting of eyebrows behind my back. I do feel some satisfaction, that as the first holder of the Phelps-Stokes fellowship, I may, to a small degree, have paved the way for others to follow, eventually accustoming the community and the State to such goings on at the University.

I was extremely fortunate at that time to have tolerant parents and doubly fortunate later to marry a woman of the same toleration, warm humanity, and impatience with intellectual dishonesty. A noncomformist on race was likely to be looked on as a renegade or "nigger lover" in the community and I can imagine that one who also lacked the full sympathy of his family would have been courting melancholia.

CHAPTER 4

Beyond the Law

I was well on the way to adolescence through a boyhood which promised to parallel that of a classmate of mine who described his early impressions in these words: "I grew up to be fifteen years old without knowing that I was any better than a nigger." When I was about twelve, however, some of the raw facts of race life burst upon me suddenly.

With a group of my contemporaries I was on the way, by horse and wagon, to a Y.M.C.A. summer camp. When we stopped in a small country town for harness repairs some of us wandered off to see what might be of local interest. A local inhabitant, with the pride of a Chamber of Commerce secretary, offered to show us something special. He led us around behind the jail and pointed to a row of fence posts. "There, boys," he said, "is where we lynched seven niggers last week. There was one in that there jail accused of rape and when the crowd went in it was dark and they warn't shore which one he was so they cleaned out the jail and took all seven that was in there and tied each one to a fence post here and shot the whole passel. That's the way we teach niggers to behave here".

I have a vivid imagination but I did not need half of it with that row of fence posts in front of me—some bullet scarred—to see the mob moving inexorably by lantern light, to hear the frantic protests followed by hopeless cries when the victims began to realize the brutality of their captors, and finally the agonized screams as the burst of gunfire cut them down. Only a small boy's dread of showing weakness enabled me to control a wave of nausea.

I remembered that I had heard some comment at the time around the streets of my home town which indicated that the better citizens thought the incident regrettable, but there did not seem to be the slightest idea that anything should be done to invoke a penalty on the mob-crazed men who had set themselves above the law by willful murder, or that anything could be done to keep the State clear of such disgraces in the future. I do not recall that any sermons were preached on the subject or that the

state dailies endeavored editorially to arouse the public conscience. Nor were they widely enough read in such isolated rural
communities to have made much of an impression, even if they
had spoken up. When, with boyish eagerness to spread news, I
tried to report to people outside my own family on what I had
seen at that row of fence posts I met a kind of shocked silence
which soon taught me that it was not fashionable to discuss such
subjects publicly. I had the feeling that even some who deplored
the incident had a sneaking suspicion that perhaps such outbreaks were necessary to make the Negro "behave himself" or, at
best, that the hearer felt that such incidents, while regrettable,
were more or less natural calamities as inevitable as thunder-
storms or cyclones. A veil of reticence enveloped the people who
might have molded public opinion. They did not stand up to
be counted.

After years of watching the lynching statistics. I believe that this
was an all-time high for the number of victims of a single mob
(if race riots are excepted). The senseless part of it was that the
man suspected of rape might not, after all, have been guilty and
that the unfortunates whose lives were snuffed out along with
his were jailed for relatively minor offenses, some no more
serious than being drunk and disorderly. They were merely un-
lucky in being in jail at the wrong time.

This may have been a record for multiple murder, but mob
killings of one, two, and three were common enough. Death by
shooting was merciful compared with some of the refinements
of cruelty invented by other mobs. Some victims were merely
crudely hanged, some emasculated first, and some converted into
human torches by soaking their clothes in kerosene—much of this
in the name of protecting the purity of Southern womanhood
but often for more trivial reasons. In the 1930's, less than a
fourth of the offences which incited lynching involved suspected
rape. From a careful first-hand study of over 100 lynchings in
the 1930's Arthur Raper, a graduate of the University of North
Carolina, concluded that probably not over two-thirds of the
alleged offenders were guilty.

The Crisis, organ of the National Association for the Advancement of Colored People, and The Negro Yearbook, a Tuskegee
Institute publication, kept painstaking records of these outrages
by verified reports and news clippings. They probably missed
some in isolated areas but the totals were shocking enough: 135

per year from 1885 to 1905, and 60 per year, during the next 20 years.

Men were not the only victims; about ten percent were women. Just how the illegal hanging of a Negro woman could protect white womanhood has never been explained. Although white people were practically the only ones lynched in the West prior to the Civil War, for a considerable period after the war, the Southern victims were almost exclusively Negro. But, as usual, when things get out of hand, those who disregarded the law began to disregard the color line, and began to lynch white people. This trend came to a climax when in 1914, a mob, enraged by the commutation of the sentence of a white man from hanging to life imprisonment, threatened the life of Governor Slaton of Georgia. Although this mob was dispersed by the militia that night another mob succeeded later in taking the prisoner from State prison officials and lynching him anyway.

Such uncontrolled madness left in its wake whole communities of demoralized, sullen, and degraded Negroes. It is debatable, however, as to whether the white South was doing more grievous hurt to the Negro or to itself by unleashing murderous passion and spitting upon the majesty of the law. As usual whenever the South goes out of the way to degrade the Negro it degrades itself and verifies the saying of Booker Washington that: "You can't hold a man in the ditch without staying there with him".

There are two plausible explanations for such irrational and barbarous behavior on the part of civilized people. One is that the perpetrators did not consider that the Negro was a human being, or if he was human, he was such a special variety that he was not elegible for American legal protection. The other is that these mobs were the symptoms of a lurking fear of the Negro, and that lynchings were not so much for the punishment of an individual as for a show of force to keep an abused people under control, a reaction to a deep subconscious fear of reprisal for abuses and indignities heaped on him before. Not that the mobsters ever reasoned these things out, for they were, for the most part, simple people not given to reasoning but acting under the urge of strong emotions.

A casual review of history is all that is necessary to demonstrate the irrationality of any such fear. The Negro is not vengeful. If he had been inclined to exact reprisal for the hardships of slavery fate presented him an unparalled opportunity when the men of the South were locked in battle with their Northern brothers, leaving only women, children, old men, and slaves behind to keep the home fires burning—but burn they did until the men in gray returned. Traditionally the Negro is more inclined to seek help from the Almighty through lamentation and prayer than to exact an eye for an eye.

There is no more perfect demonstration of this reliance on prayer than was found in the tactics of the Negroes of Montgomery, Alabama, in their reliance on prayer and passive resistance to escape from the impasse of their bus strike even though such meek protest was answered by harassment, indictment, and conviction on the ground that they withheld their dimes from the bus company.

But lynching was only the most spectacular of the extra-legal brutalities. For every lynching there were dozens of unreported non-fatal insults, damage to property, or beatings. Certain elements in the South were so busy keeping the Negro 'in his place' that they forgot that the South was supposed to be a courteous, law-abiding, tolerant American region.

Whipping had been a legal means of disciplining slaves and it was adopted illegally by those landlords who did not have the wit to control otherwise. Not far from my uncle Harvie's plantation a "cracker" whom we will give the alias of Butch Carmody had a small three-tenant farm. I could tell from the tone and expression of my elders whenever the subject of Butch was mentioned that they would have preferred it if he had settled in some other neighborhood. It was not uncommon in passing his place to hear the howls and whacks which floated down to the road as the harness strap was applied to bare, black buttocks.

As is usual when a custom is prevalent among the folk, stories grow about it. One of these which passed as humor at the time concerned an alleged incident of a man in a South Georgia town who shot a Negro and was haled into police court and fined ten dollars for discharging firearms within the city limits.

A Negro was afraid to press his end of a business transaction too vigorously. He had to be extraordinarily careful not to jostle the wrong person on the sidewalk inadvertently. In some communities he never knew whether if, under the exuberant influence of illegal corn drippings, he lost control of his language he might sober up in Abraham's bosom.

Such brutalities could not have been so widespread if law

officers and jurors had been determined to put a stop to them. But the law officers were put there by the electors who were the voters in the white Democratic primary. Without the protection afforded by the power to vote and serve on juries, the Negro was helpless.

Interracial violence flourished most in backward rural communities—small, isolated counties where the law enforcement machinery was weak. It could, however, flare up anywhere with startling suddenness if the passions of the mob got out of hand before the law officers got on the job. This seems to have been the case in the recent outbreak on the campus of the University of Alabama. The campus was quiet and no one in authority was aware of the witches' brew of stories and rumors which were circulating under the surface to be brought to a head with disconcerting speed by a few hotheaded leaders.

Superheated friction arising from racial disputes worked itself off differently in cities. Here it culminated in race riots far more bloody but less common than lynchings. DuBois records 19 riots in 1919. These were more frequent in the North. East St. Louis, Chicago, Detroit, Harlem, and even the Nation's Capitol at one time or another were affected. This has been cited by the South as a justification of its own record, but to point the finger elsewhere and say 'thou too' is the sorriest sort of defense.

Lynching, in part, was a flareback of the summary justice of the early Western frontier and, in part, a survival of the regulatory code of the Ku Klux. Extralegal measures for settling race disputes became less common as the influence of these factors faded. It is not possible to put a finger on any one event which marked the beginning of the end of violence. Gradually leaders began to speak up, the level of rural education was raised, and sheriffs began to stiffen their backbones. The end is not yet. As long as the two races live side by side there is always the possibility that personal disagreements will heat tempers to the point of explosion, but now anyone who takes the law into his own hands is far more apt to be punished by the law than he was in 1900.

Slowly, almost grudgingly, the habit of violent settlement of disputes was loosening its talons from the South. In the years immediately preceding Word War I lynchings still averaged nearly sixty a year. It required constant and concentrated action by many people and many organizations to reduce it to four in the years preceding World War II and it was not until 1952 that the page had no blots. Since lynching may be considered the most aggravated symptom of the disease of violence, and since it was conquered by efforts to strengthen respect for the law and create public opinion, other forms of violence have followed a similar downward trend in most sections of the South.

This is the darkest phase of race relations, the Gehenna for which the South has been flayed by the North, and for which America has been castigated by Communists at home and abroad and because of which, our potential friends in the colored nations around the world have set little store by the professed ideals of American democracy. It may, therefore, be worthwhile to review the record by underlining the fact that the most lurid examples of interracial violence which are the favorite weapons of their propaganda are, with occasional exceptions, things of the past and, if present trends continue, may forever be relegated to its dark pages.

The South's own efforts to win this battle are bright pages in its history. That is not to say that outside pressures were not a spur to these efforts. I do not intend to minimize the effect of the propaganda campaigns and pressure for anti-lynching legislation by the National Association for the Advancement of Colored People or other outside organizations. Without them as a spur the South would not have moved so rapidly. I shall, however, speak mostly of the movement with which I was actively associated for six years following 1920—the Commission on Interracial Cooperation.

Immediately after World War I, the South was a region of rumors and alarms. Forgotten was the wartime pride in the willingness of the Negro to serve in the armed forces, his contribution in proportion to his means to war loans and patriotic drives, his prodigies of production in the shipyards and munitions plants. In its place was a vague apprehension for what the troops might do after they came from experiences different from the Southern tradition. Deep down the South was worried by the wartime ditty:

> *"How're you going to keep 'em down on the farm . . . after they've seen Paree?"*

A group of opportunists saw in this disturbed state of mind an opportunity to make a fast dollar. Shouting "white supremacy" they organized the twentieth century edition of the Ku Klux Klan with all is infantile trappings of klaverns and kleagles, its uniform consisting of a two-dollar night shirt for which the initiate paid the Klan officials ten dollars. So many of these robes were sold that the Klan set up a thriving robe factory. Its activities were a perfect outlet for the frustration of many unimportant men who amounted to little in the community and were probably much henpecked at home. Behind the anonymity of a peaked hood they could assert themselves. They could, with impunity, parade their supremacy over Negros, Catholics and Jews. The latter two hates earned them more converts in the other regions than in the South for the few Jewish families in the South were well established, respected citizens. There were also few Catholics outside of Louisiana so this was a group which could also be hated without fear of reprisal.

Although the hate of the Catholics which the Ku Klux managed to stir up was hate of the unknown, it was widespread enough to cause several Southern States, in 1928, to vote Republican for the first time since the Civil War because the Democratic candidate, Al Smith, was of the Catholic faith.

But their pet hate was the Negro. They left no room for doubt that the chief object of their nocturnal parades and fiery crosses was to intimidate and terrorize the colored man who had been led to believe that he had just done a pretty good job of cooperating with his white brothers in making the world safe for democracy.

Unlike the post-Civil War South, the Twentieth Century South had more level-headed leaders whose hearts could not hate and whose respect for the law was too deep to allow it to be travestied by self-appointed regulators without protest. They organized. In doing so they injected something new. They associated with themselves outstanding Negro leaders and, for the first time, gave these men a respectable platform from which they could feel free to express their hopes and their frustrations frankly and know that they would get a sympathetic hearing and, if it were possible, some redress. A later chapter will give more detail as to the philosophy and mechanics of this organization, known as the Commission on Interracial Cooperation. Here we are chiefly concerned with their campaign against violence.

Very early it was apparent to these men that an attack on violence had to be threefold: south-wide, state-wide and county-wide.

South-wide it was the commission's job to line up powerful allies such as religious denominations, YMCA and YWCA, universities, womens' organizations, business men, editorial associations, and any other sympathetic groups. This was a focal point from which a systematic attack on public opinion could be directed and systematic constructive activities planned. Nothing less than such intensive cultivation of the seeds of goodwill could have been so effective.

At first these pioneers were few in number but strong in faith. When it became known that some of the South's respected leaders were willing to take action in the face of hostility, more allies joined. The application of the principles of Christian brotherhood to the colored brothers was more often advocated in pulpits, and the disgrace of violence was more frequently the subject of editorials. Some fifty thousand Southern women signed a petition against lynching, letting it be known that they did not seek the type of protection which mob rule claimed to give them. Local law officers, feeling for the first time, that they had moral support for courageous action, dispersed mobs more frequently. In short, on the subject of violence, the South began to come to its senses. Southern leaders began to try to square their ideas of justice with the traditional American ideal of equality under the law for all.

Nor did the effort come too soon. Negroes in and out of the armed services had learned that there are other places in which they could live and be relatively secure. The great migration northward which started before the war to escape the boll weevil continued after the war to escape lack of protection, intimidation, and brutality. Between 1910 and 1930 the number of Negroes living outside the South increased by a million and a quarter. They had begun to exercise the one effective protest that they had discovered, namely, to move out of the mess.

After 1900, when neighboring states were running up a heavy lynching score, hotheaded South Carolina was exceptionally free from mob fatalities. This is probably attributable, at least in part, to the fact that they placed a law on their statute book permitting the family of a mob victim to sue a county in which a lynching occurred, placing the burden of proof on the local officials to show that they had not been negligent.

Since state police organizations were non-existent, the whole burden of prevention of violent action or apprehension and prosecution of perpetrators of illegal acts rested on local officials, locally elected by the white voters. The main push for elimination of racial outbreaks, therefore, had to be made in the counties by a grass roots effort to brace up the sagging structure of law enforcement. It had to be genuinely a grass roots operation because a stranger making inquiries in one of these small isolated communities stood out like a sore thumb and his activities were closely followed by members of the Ku Klux and in some cases he was threatened by local bullies. Anyone from another State or even another county was subject to this suspicion and unless he had local sponsorship he might as well stay out, for local officials would pay him scant attention.

Local sponsorship was secured in many Southern counties through local interracial committees. The success or failure of these committees depended entirely on the calibre of local leaders who could be persuaded to serve. But regardless of the strength of the committee members, the fact that any white people would intervene in behalf of a Negro gave some pause to the lawless element.

Some of the most active cooperation came from employers of Negro labor. In addition to the personal interest which many of these men felt in their workers, it began to dawn on them that the very economic underpinning of the region was under attack. They were fed up with the periodic intimidation and demoralization of their labor force.

People began to discover that mobs could be frustrated in various ways. The standard procedure of sheriffs who were in earnest and had sufficient time was to take their prisoner to a jail in another county where passions had not been roused. A Negro mob was broken up in an ingenious manner. The story goes that some miscreant had committed a particularly brutal crime against a Negro woman. Since she was well respected in the community, two mobs, one white and one colored were out to beat the sheriff to the capture. The white mob found him first but as a matter of protocol turned him over to the Negro mob as their meat. The prospective victim, however, was shrewd enough to capitalize on his knowledge of psychology and obtained permission to make a final prayer. His prayer was such a long, loud, and eloquent plea for the orderly processes of the law and for the sinful souls of his would-be lynchers that the assembly began to pray with him and, on second thought, decided to take him to the sheriff.

John Steelman, later top labor adviser to Presidents Roosevelt and Truman, had an experience with a budding Ku Klux mob which was not without its ridiculous overtones. At the time he was Professor of Sociology at Alabama State College but was spending some time in investigating outbreaks of violence for the Interracial Commission. He had interviewed a number of people of Tuscaloosa about a recent incident and it did not take long for the word to get around that a stranger was sticking his nose where strange noses might smell too much. One night just before retiring he was visited at his hotel by the local Ku Klux in their fantastic regalia of robes and hoods. They probably had some vague notion of throwing such a scare into John that he would leave town, but he didn't scare easily.

It was a terribly hot night, humid to the stifling point, so by the time the deputation reached the hotel under the heavy robes and hoods they were pretty well melted down. John was in his pajamas and reasonably comfortable with a fan going. He prolonged their misery by refusing at first to grant their demand that they be allowed to come in and examine the contents of his briefcase, on the theory that a man's hotel room is his castle. Finally, when he felt that they had sweated off enough of their steam, he said:

"Well boys, I don't want you to stew there all night so come on in and I'll show you some literature." It so happened that his briefcase was full of nothing more than the term papers of his sociology students. Some of the papers were on the subject The New Deal and the Ku Kluxers were very interested and suspicious. The sweating therefore continued while the deputation tried to figure out just what this queer subversive literature was.

After they had given it up as hopeless they wanted John to go down and unlock his car so they could examine it also. John gave them another lecture about the sanctity of private property and closed by making this proposition: "I will let you go through my car if you will agree to assemble your whole group (who were waiting outside) and let me make them a talk". They agreed and so John soon had his turn at bat. He stood on the railroad platform near the hotel and soon some three hundred had assembled. He told them many facts about Tuscaloosa, and about Alabama—facts which would hardly have been known to a "foreigner". He pointed out how silly it looked for grown men to be playing spooks and reminded them that their wives were wondering where they were and imagining all sorts of possibilities such as card games or beer parties. That did it. The Klan sneaked back to their Klavern, shed their robes and hurried home before the good wife could really get angry.

Men who had been beaten, shot at, or otherwise terrorized began to find their way to the headquarters of the Interracial Commission in search of help. After listening to many, it was decided that a few strategic prosecutions were needed. Ex-governor Hugh Dorsey generously offered his assistance in prosecuting cases which promised to get some results, advocating the philosophy that one thrust of the bayonet was worth a thousand metaphysical speculations on the art of warfare.

An opportunity to thrust the bayonet soon came. A quiet, earnest Negro, Asbury McClusky, about fifty years of age, told us this story: He owned a medium-sized, fairly successful farm in a nearby county and had tried to get along as best he could with his neighbors, paying his debts and tending his crops. He had never had any trouble until recently, and had expected none. A short time before when, as he expressed it, the Klux began to ride, he had heard some growls from the rougher element to the effect that they did not like "uppity niggers". He paid no serious attention to them at the time.

Suddenly, however, a mob appeared at his home in the dead of night and demanded that he come out and be whipped. "I told them", said Asbury, that "no man had ever whipped me and no man wus going to". He still thought they were probably some rowdy drunks who would bluff some more and go on off but some of them began firing pistols into his front door. That was when he went back for his shotgun. "I yelled to them that I had a gun and would use it if they didn't stop shooting in the house where my wife and children were." After one or two more shots while Asbury was "squinched up against the wall" he fired hitting one, whom we will call Joe Morgan, in the leg. They all left then to drive Joe to the hospital. In a few days Asbury left, too, for the safer climate of Atlanta. We cross questioned him at length and his story never varied. It had the unmistakable ring of truth. It had been bright moonlight. There was a glass panel in his door and before the firing had started he was very sure he had recognized Joe Morgan and Jim Snipes, since the mob had not even troubled to wear masks.

The more we probed, the more it became clear that the attack on Asbury was the climax of a series of such outrages in that one county. He produced Willie Peters who had been driven off his small patch of land and forced to sacrifice it for a ridiculous price; and Uncle Sweet Lay, an inoffensive middle-aged man, who had been whipped. Gradually, we pieced together the shameful picture of a whole community terrorized by a band of irresponsible roughnecks operating anonymously. People who were not members of the Ku Klux never knew but what their neighbor might be a member. They were reluctant to talk for fear they might be next on the whipping list. Within the span of five months, five white men and seven Negroes had been shot, beaten, or driven off. It was almost as bad as the South Side of Chicago when gangsters ruled unchecked.

The one public official who showed his indignation was the Circuit Judge. He was a resident of an adjoining county and in spite of the fact that these marauders included a substantial number of the voters to whom he would soon appeal for reelection he wanted to exert his full power to uphold the law in his circuit. But a judge is powerless to act until a grand jury has brought an indictment and the accused is brought into court. The judge warned us that we would not secure a conviction or even an indictment in that county as long as the juries were packed with members of the Ku Klux.

Governor Dorsey's contention was that we did not need a conviction if we could get an indictment and get these men in open court out from under their hoods so the law abiding people could get a good look at the sorry specimens of whom they had been afraid.

I went down and nosed around and, on a tip from Asbury, found a country merchant who had joined the Klan but pulled out in disgust. He knew every local member and was afraid of nobody. He promised: "If the judge will put me on the commission which selects the names of voters chosen for jury service I will clean every Kluxer out of the jury box". The Judge appointed him and he carried out his promise but was beaten up for his boldness. Still he told the world in no uncertain terms what had happened and for the first time, now that they had no friends on the jury, fear of the law gnawed at the complacency of the mobsters. The grand jury did indict the two who had been identified and they were tried.

Ordinarily, court week attracted a good audience in these communities which had few recreation facilities but when the word got around that an ex-Governor, for whom many of them had voted, was to assist the prosecution the house was packed. As we had expected, we secured no conviction. The only witnesses which the prosecution could produce were Negroes. The white buddies of the defendants rallied around with perfect alibis. According to their story, Joe Morgan had shot himself accidentally while cleaning his gun, and Jim Snipes could not have been at Asbury's house at the time alleged because he was with the crowd on Main Street when the Seaboard express blew for the crossing. They were defended by the most prominent local lawyer who had political ambitions. They got off, but they had been given a very healthy scare and made to stand up in court so that everybody could see what manner of men they were. The community was cured. For a number of years thereafter it was as orderly as a Sunday School class.

This was not the only trial. Later, the members of a county interracial committee, without outside aid, secured convictions and jail sentences for four mob members. Thus the battle went on for three decades with lawlessness slowly but steadily losing ground. After the Interracial Commission got into full stride in 1925 the annual average of lynchings dropped precipitously to 5 per year and now they rarely occur. The time has not yet come however, for completely relaxed complacency since there are still some backward communities where violence goes unpunished. On the whole, however, the South has shown that it can cope effectively with race friction when it has really made up its mind.

CHAPTER 5

Sharecroppers Arrive

The grim necessity of finding a new formula for living and working together was staring both ex-master and ex-slave in the face at the close of the Civil War. Gone were many of the personal relationships which had approximated family ties. Released from the compulsion to work at the direction of the master, the freedman no longer had someone to do his thinking and planning, to help him through poor crop years, to look after him in time of illness. It was clearly imperative to work out new economic and personal arrangements. The new pattern which emerged was naturally as close to the old as was consistent with the new legal status, for customs which have crystallized over generations are not changed by a proclamation and it is human to cleave to the familiar rather than risk the unknown. This new device was sharecropping.

The only things which stood between both colored and white and abject poverty were the willingness to work and the availability of land, much of which had been shamefully abused by continuous cultivation of cotton or tobacco without conservation practices, many planters considering it cheaper to desert run-down lands than to conserve the soil.

The cropper plantation was modeled after the slave plantation and evolved from a network of dependencies. In the Lower South both tenant and landowner were bound to cotton partly by custom and partly by lack of markets for other crops. Fortunately, cotton was a bonanza in the early years. The Southeast still had a virtual monopoly on its production and the demand piled up during the war sent the price skyrocketing to about eighty cents per pound in 1866.

The economics of poverty also bound the two races together. Cotton was the only source of cash income. The crop requires heavy doses of hand labor and the landholders could secure labor only from ex-slaves. The ex-slaves had to have a way to eat without money and the landlord was the only hope for this credit. It was necessary to evolve a system under which they could cooperate in the production of cotton with the minimum of friction.

38

The system of cash wages was not feasible for landlords who were not in a position to supervise their operations closely nor was it too acceptable to the newly freed Negro because of the strictness of supervision involved. In describing what took place in 1865 and 1866 R. P. Brooks, an agricultural economist, wrote:

"On many plantations operations went ahead with scarcely any interruption. Planters called informal meetings of the freedmen, explained in simple terms their new condition and offered employment at the current rate of wages to all who desired to remain. After wandering off a short distance simply to assert their new freedom many Negroes returned to the plantation and took up their former labor. Those planters who had been most considerate of their slaves experienced the least trouble in employing them as freedmen . . .

"On the other hand there was a large element of the freedmen who did not follow the course just outlined. The widespread belief that the plantations of their former owners would be divided among the ex-slaves at Christmas 1865, acted as a deterrent to steady industry. The Commissioner of the Freedmen's Bureau found it necessary to send out special instructions to all officers and agents, directing them to do what they could to dispel this delusion."

Concerning conditions in 1866 General Howell Cobb, a Georgia operator of large plantations, observed:

"I find things worse with the Negroes than I expected, and am unable to say what we shall be able to do. From Nathan Barwick's place every negro has left. There is no one to feed the stock, and on the other places none have contracted as yet. . . . I am offering them even better terms than I gave them last year, to wit: one-third of the cotton and corn crop, and they feed and clothe themselves, but nothing satisfies them. Grant them one thing and they demand something more, and there is no telling where they would stop. The truth is, I am thoroughly disgusted with free negro labor, and determined that the next year shall close my operations with them. Old Ellick stayed out in the woods and sent for the negroes and they were bargaining with him in the night and telling Barwick in the day that they were going to stay with him. The moment that they got their money, they started for the railroad. Among them was Anderson, son of Sye and Sentry, whom I am supporting at "Hurricane."

It will be noted in this letter that General Cobb had not progressed beyond offering his tenants more than one-third of the crop. This never was satisfactory and the sharing arrangement which became the standard was for the tenant to get one-half or two-thirds of the crop depending on how much of the operating capital he furnished. Still other planters rented their lands outright rather than be burdened with the irritation and risk involved in dealing with free labor. The full transition is traced by D. C. Barrow, a former Chancellor of the University of Georgia, in describing his family plantation:

"For several years following emancipation the force of laborers was divided into two squads, the arrangement and method of cultivation was very much as in the ante-bellum period. Each squad was under an overseer, or foreman. The hands were given a share of the crop. As the time went on, the control of the foreman became irksome to the Negroes. As a consequence the squads were split up into smaller and smaller groups, still working for part of the crop and still using the owners teams. The process of disintegration continued until each laborer worked separately, without any oversight. The change involved great loss and trouble. Mules were ill treated, the crop was badly worked, and often tenants stole the landlord's share. It became necessary to abandon the sharing feature. The owner sold his mules to the tenants, thereby putting on them the burden of loss. . . . The negroes now planted what they pleased and worked when they liked, the landlord interfering only to require that enough cotton be planted to pay the rent."

Thus, some landlords were able to continue production with wage labor; some rented out their lands but the majority adopted some sharing system allowing the tenant one-half, two-thirds or three-fourths of the proceeds of the crop, depending on how much working capital the tenant could furnish and how much of the risk of loss he was willing to assume.

The desire for prestige alone kept many landlords in the business. Before the Civil War society had been dominated by large planters and they controlled the major portion of the wealth. This prestige of the planter carried over in the South after the War to such an extent that many men who were not capable of successful farming held on to land. They were willing to stay land poor if only they could eke out enough income to pay taxes on the family inheritance long after they had moved away leaving the operation to renters who had no incentive to conserve soil or maintain buildings which they did not own.

Tenants were equally dependent upon landowners. They had been freed from physical bondage but not prepared for the impersonal insecurities of free competition. They became part of an economy where disaster could strike through sudden illness, crop failure, fire or theft, or even the death of their mainstay, the mule. They started, for the most part, without tangible assets. The more fortunate might have had a few sticks of furniture taken over from slave cabins, one or two primitive cooking utensils, and perhaps an iron pot for boiling clothes. For several generations one of the most accurate measures of the economic progress of a tenant family was the acquisition of a cook stove.

The benevolent government, which had freed them, sent them forth with less than the suit of clothes and transportation money which we now give a discharged convict. Having salved his New England conscience by the grand gesture of emancipation followed by reconstruction the liberator dismissed the Southern economy from further concern under the bland assumption that the mess left by the war was the sole concern of the South. Quite true the Freedmen's Bureau was established with high sounding objectives for assisting the ex-slaves. During its existence, however, it disbursed only twenty million dollars, or an average of five dollars per freedman, including the staggering overhead involved in carrying a corps of bureaucratic administrators, many of whom were far more interested in promoting their political or financial future by continuing the subjection of the White South than they were in advancing the economic welfare of the Negro. The policies of this ill-starred organization were such that the White South was bitterly alienated, thus destroying any chance for cooperation in working out a mutually acceptable governmental program. As a result, after 1869, the Freedmen's Bureau was no more. Its one contribution which was of continuing benefit to the Negro was the establishment of some free public schools and some substantial colleges which still continue to make a valuable contribution to the college education of Negroes. But in this case also the antagonism of the White South to anything associated with the Freedman's Bureau was transferred in large measure to these schools which otherwise were deserving of the wholehearted support of their locality.

The Southern white man and Southern Negro recognizing, therefore, that what happened in the South would not be further concern of the Northern zealots (at least for some years), hitched up their belts and continued to do what they were accustomed to do. Former slaveholders became the landlords and former slaves became wage hands or sharecroppers, often remaining in the same house they had occupied during slavery. Some few were helped to modest property ownership by those former masters who could afford it. Others who had been trained as artisans moved into town. The vast majority, however, remained on the land.

This mutual dependence manifested itself in strange ways. Booker Washington tells of a Negro gardener whose work habits frequently irritated his hot-tempered employer to such a pitch that he was fired. But after a few days layoff he would be rehired only to be refired later. Finally the employer boiled over and told him never to show his face on the place again. Next day, however, he was back on the job before his employer was even out of bed. When this was discovered the employer exploded: "I thought I told you to stay away from here". The Negro replied: "Boss, I'm not going to quit a good job every time you get mad."

The races were not only dependent upon cotton and upon each other but both were slaves of debt. I still have among my souveniers a few Confederate bills which my grandfather gave me as part of the capital he had left after the war. He had long since disposed of the repudiated Confederate bonds. But he and a handful of others were fortunate in that they had professions to fall back on even though their income also was derived mostly from a depressed farm economy.

The deficit in capital was not made up by the few years of high-priced cotton in the late 1860's, for unsettled conditions reduced crop yields to about one hundred and sixty pounds per acre—less than they have ever been since except in the 1920's when boll weevil damage was catastrophic. Also post-war inflation pushed all prices to fantastic levels so that income from the cotton crop passed through the farmers' hands and little stuck. Soon after 1870 the price of cotton was back below ten cents per pound, ranging in some years down to six cents. It stayed below ten cents until after 1910. In normal years, with cotton bringing close to ten cents, the farmers could barely make buckle and tongue meet. With the price close to six cents, landlord and tenant both faced privation.

The new South had to finance its recovery on credit and started out a year behind in money and barely two days ahead of the sheriff. By the time that the Eastern banks had taken their cut of

interest, and the Southern banks or merchants had subtracted
theirs, and the landlord his, the income which filtered down to the
cropper was meager indeed.

Land was not acceptable as a basis for credit. So much land
was up for distress sales that it was a drug on the market. Brooks
cites a single issue of a Georgia daily which advertised twenty-six
thousand acres for sale and he notes one sale of four-hundred acres
at ten cents per acre and two others one of four-hundred acres and
the other of two-hundred, which sold for the lump sum of two
dollars and a half apiece. A mortgage on a future crop was the
usual collateral offered as the security for the advance of the expenses of growing the crop and eating during the crop season.

Theoretically the sharecrop system was a method by which a
landless, moneyless man could produce by having his expenses
advanced at the beginning of the year by the landlord or merchant
and deducted from his share of the crop when it was marketed.
Theoretically also, after some years in this status, he would be
able to accumulate capital to buy his own mule, plows, seeds, and
fertilizer and finance his living expenses, thus climbing the agricultural ladder to the status of independent renter and eventually
to land-ownership. From the landlord's viewpoint it was a means
of securing labor for at least one crop season, deferring the full
wage payment until the crop was marketed, and escaping part of
it if the marketed crop did not cover such amounts as had been
advanced. From the tenant's viewpoint it was designed to stimulate
production of a crop through a financial interest in its success.

Since, however, the system was one of human relationships it
did not always work that way. It was subject to abuses by both
parties, especially by the landlord, since he controlled the amount
of advances, the rate of interest charged, and the sale of the crop.
There were sharp dealings by both parties, so much so that many
stories circulated among the folk. One of these concerns a tenant
who brought three bales of cotton to his landlord after harvest to
settle accounts. The landlord consulted a dog-eared ledger and
seemingly performed the arithmetic of crediting the tenant's half
of the cotton at a theoretical price and making various deductions
for feed, seed, fertilizer and living expenses which had been ad-

"John" he said, "We came out exactly even but I am going to
give you a present of five dollars."

"Boss" said John, "Are you shore we are even?"

"Of course, John, you are not questioning my accounts, are you?"

"Oh no boss. It shore is good, cause I got two more bales left out home".

"You son of a gun, John, why didn't you tell me that? Now I have got to figure this all over again".

Another avenue for a particularly blatant type of exploitation was opened by the so-called peonage laws which made it a misdemeanor to leave a contract while in debt. These laws were originally passed to protect the landlord against tenants who might receive advances for several months, secured by a growing crop, and then quit in the middle of the season leaving the crop to the weeds. These were soon made the excuse by unprincipled landlords to keep the tenant in debt by various devices and threaten his arrest if he tried to change jobs, thus bringing back a modified type of slavery.

There were landlords of all degrees of ability and fairness and there were tenants of all degrees of diligence and honesty. To quote again from *The Negro Landholder in Georgia* by Dubois: "A thrifty Negro in the hands of well-disposed landlords and honest merchants early became an independent landowner. A shiftless, ignorant Negro in the hand of unscrupulous landlords or shylocks became something worse than a slave. The masses of Negroes between the two extremes fared as chance and the weather let them."

Thus the agricultural ladder was not a one-way street. The rungs were greased with difficulties and some of the climbers were weak, fainthearted or apathetic. There were some who succeeded but there were many who failed and slipped back while some fell off the ladder completely.

In characterizing movement up the ladder as "progress", it is well to keep in mind that the rungs were unequal. A climb to some was relatively simple as in the case of the step from wage laborer to sharecropper. Others were quite difficult as in the case of progress from cropper to renter or owner. In any case the higher the perch the more precarious the hold.

The difference between working for wages and working for half the crop profits was nominal. According to the statutes and the rulings, the cropper was a laborer. He had no title to his crop in many states, only a laborer's lien which stood after that of the landlord or credit merchant.

Another vicious effect of the share crop system, however, arose from the fact that the tenant had no reimbursable interest in the improvements which he might make. He got nothing for either conserving or improving land, equipment or buildings. Small wonder then that the soil washed away, the work stock deteriorated, and houses became hardly fit for habitation. I had a friend who traveled extensively in the Southeast who claimed that the miracle which was needed most to improve the looks of the section was to have a rain of paint.

There was one slightly encouraging trend. Despite the disadvantages and discouragements, a few Negroes had managed to become independent owners. By 1910 these numbered 220,000. The slow growth of this class has, by many apologists, been blamed on the obstacles to land ownership raised by the system and by white opposition. Although land was to be had at bargain prices certain attitudes and characteristics of the Negro hampered his advance. The majority of Negroes were not far enough from slavery to have developed a deep-seated land hunger or the thrift and foresight necessary for saving. The constant din of propaganda against agriculture as a way of life which was carried on by the Negro intelligentsia had also soured many Negroes on farming as a career and others were deterred by the the relatively greater insecurity in rural areas.

Many of the Negroes who did become farm owners were graduates of Hampton, Tuskegee, and the smaller agricultural schools but the majority were self-taught farmers. The Southern States were shirking their obligation to give thorough agricultural training although they had subscribed to this obligation in principle. For a variety of reasons the majority of Negro farmers missed a golden opportunity to become independent owners.

The two hundred and twenty thousand owners in 1910 were the peak number. The boll weevil dislocated some of these and the attraction of city life took others away from the land so that by the onset of the depression Negro farm ownership had declined by about one-fifth. In 1954, the number of Negro farm owners was about the same as in 1930 but they constituted a far larger proportion of all Negro farmers.

True, the Negro landowner was no longer under the thumb of the landlord or subject to his whims but he had other troubles. Many of the tracts owned were too small to be efficient and many consisted of poor land since white people were extremely reluctant to sell to Negroes in good-land areas. Above all, however, he was still subject to the usurious credit system. If he could not raise money on his land or livestock he had to offer a crop mortgage as security and pay as high as 30 per cent interest. One farmer who had just negotiated a crop loan from the bank was asked whether he realized the interest he was paying and he said, no, but that he knew that borrowing money from Mr. B. was like burning down your house to get warm. "It gives no permanent relief."

As handicapped as they were, these owners were still in a more advantaged position to benefit by the post-depression recovery programs than the croppers. It would be interesting to compare the condition of the 1950 Negro owners with those of 1930, but that research remains to be done.

I was town-reared and my earliest firsthand view of plantation life came during summer visits to Uncle Harvie's Middle-Georgia acres. His father and his father's father had been planters and he was doing his best to follow their lead. True to tradition his house had high white columns, beautiful mantels, and ornamented ceilings which were the product of skilled slave artisans. It was set back from the winding, unsurfaced clay road about three miles from town. His tenants lived on the lower place several miles in the other direction. They were not in evidence except when they came up for supplies or to have help with some problem. His head man, George, did live close by and George's wife, Caroline, presided over the kitchen.

The main attraction for me was a couple of cousins about my own age, ideal summer companions. Also adding to the spice of life was an assortment of Negro playmates about the same age. We did not "spend the night" as kids do now nor share the same table but nothing inhibited our interracial raids on Aunt Caroline's supply of fat biscuits which we would embellish by poking a hole in the side and filling with 'lasses. We could also top these off by finding where the plumpest blackberries were ripening or where the sweetest peaches were ready to pick. Sometimes an especially outrageous prank would provoke a mass switching, each parent chastising her own. I am not aware that this enjoyment of interracial fun did me any harm or undermined the Southern way of life as some now fear would result from interracial contacts in public recreation.

In retrospect, I imagine that my uncle's plantation was as near like that of his father as he could make it except for the arrangements with his labor. Cotton was about the only cash crop. Corn was produced as food for animals and humans. He had a well-tended garden, good hogs, cows and plenty of poultry. He also took interest in the gardens of those of his tenants who could be persuaded to plant them. In some respects he was an innovator, an incessant reader of progressive farm publications always in search of new ideas. Queer crops appeared from time to time. He tried Elberta peaches early in the game but this too was a chancy crop. We were one time delighted to have a pair of Angora goats to amuse us. I don't know what became of that experiment but I imagine central Georgia had no market for mohair. Geese and turkeys were around for home consumption, the latter being somewhat uncommon, so much so, that one of my cousins disappeared about dusk one night and was found doing his best to roost with them on the garden fence. Sugar cane and peanuts would and did grow. One of the few things which he did not experiment with was tobacco. All of these were not so much the projects of a dreamer but efforts to be self-sufficient and find a way out of the bondage of cotton. In a region where a bewildering variety of products could be grown, lack of intelligent labor and absence of profitable markets nullified his efforts. His fields were terraced, that being the extent of soil conservation practice at the time. The only green cover crop I saw was black-eyed peas.

His relations with tenants were amicable and I think fair, but of necessity strict, which meant that the ablest tenants were eager to work on his place. His desk drawer had a box of nickles, dimes, and quarters which never circulated except on Sunday when it was parceled out to the tenants to tote to church and jingle in their pockets so they could brag that tenants on his place always had money. It was always promptly returned on Monday.

I do not know how many other Uncle Harvies there were in the Cotton Belt trying to find a better system of production but I do know that it was at least four decades before a more profitable way of eking money out of land was found except in limited areas. He finally gave up and moved to Atlanta partly because of the uphill struggle with cotton and partly because the limited contacts and advantages which were furnished by plantation life were not what he wanted for his growing family.

The sharecrop plantation was typical of Southern agriculture by 1880 and continued with little modification until the great depression began to loosen the cake of custom. It dominated the life of the Cotton South. It controlled the economics of the region and also, through the prestige of the planters, it set the fashions in race relations which carried over into the new cities and still persist stubbornly in some areas, although the conditions by which they were shaped have changed.

Both races found in this institution a framework within which they could cooperate in the poor man's occupation of cotton culture. The Negro had established a foothold, especially in share-cropping, which in many respects was superior to slavery. A few had become independent owners and renters of small farms. In the early decades nearly all the tenants were Negroes. Soon, however, white tenants appeared; by 1930 they were one and one-half times as numerous as Negro tenants.

Up to 1930, in spite of the drab life, tenancy increased. Just before the turn of the century only about one-third of the Southern farms were operated by tenants but, by 1930, the proportion had increased to one-half. As we shall see in the next chapter the trend was reversed by the depression and World War II so that tenancy in the South was back down to thirty percent in 1954.

At the peak a million and three-quarters farm families were squeezing out a hard living as cotton and tobacco tenants and it was this situation which was largely responsible for characterization of the region by Franklin Roosevelt as Economic Problem Number One.

CHAPTER 6

Sharecroppers (and Mules) Depart

Though stunning in its impact, the great depression was little more than an exaggeration of the ups and downs which cash-crop farming had suffered for decades. The basic weaknesses of the system were well known. Journals had been harping on them for many years. The more intelligent farmers were becoming aware of the trap they were in, but they were hypnotized by cash-crop gambles as a bird by a snake. The credit system was such that they were compelled to produce for the market no matter how wastefully. They knew that ignorance and inertia were at the root of many of their troubles but that only time and better schools could cure that. They were beginning to realize that cotton farming was no more than a set of inherited motions. A Northern visitor to a Mississippi plantation is reputed to have watched the automatic motions of the cotton pickers for a while and suggested to the employer that, since it would appear that monkeys could be trained to do such work, some should be imported for this purpose. After the employer had thought the matter over for a while he observed: "No it wouldn't work. As soon as we got them trained you Yankees would come down here and set them free."

Most farmers knew that slavish dependence on cotton or tobacco was a tricky gamble where the risk was largely carried by the poor man who could least afford it. But deaf ears were turned to the suggestion:

> *A garden and a cow*
> *A smokehouse and a sow*
> *Twenty-four hens and a rooster*
> *And you will have more than you used'ter*

Instead some landlords facetiously claimed that their tenants wanted houses built high off the ground so they could plant cotton under them not just up to them. They realized that there were too many people on the land, that this bred unemployment, under-employment, and waste of labor, but where else could

49

they go? They knew that more machinery, and more scientific fertilization and better varieties of seed would increase income but were held back by lack of capital and ignorance of labor. They could see their main asset, the top soil, washing away, turning the rivers red with silt. By 1933, one-third of the crop land in the South was seriously eroded and over half of the eroded land of the nation was in the South. But soil conservation was expensive, either requiring cash outlays or the planting of crops which would not produce immediate returns.

Notwithstanding this knowledge the system did not change until it felt the effects of the revolution in American farming which accompanied the efforts to crawl out of the depression and later to remold the labor force to meet the demands of a booming industry.

Awareness of these needs of the Southern farmer led Seaman and Bradford Knapp, of Arkansas, to initiate the farm demonstration service. First with the backing of the General Education Board and later with Federal support these farmers' friends spread through the South and into the rest of the nation becoming the Agricultural Extension Service. The best these men could do, at first, however, was to exhort and demonstrate, gradually spreading the doctrine of scientific agriculture to a few progressive farmers and to boys' and girls' clubs. They could only reach the plantation tenant by permission of the landlord and most of these were unsympathetic with diversification and production for home use.

And how had King Cotton and Queen Tobacco rewarded the loyalty of their subjects? The depression found millions of them illiterate, debt ridden, poverty stricken, living in shacks, subsisting on a meagre diet, with world competition weakening their monopoly on cotton and competition coming at home from synthetic fibres.

Landlords were almost as hard hit by the depression as tenants. They were still heavily dependent upon credit, and the sources of credit had dried up. They were uncertain about trying to raise cotton when the price threatened to go through the floor. They were forced to tell their tenants that they could no longer advance them money to live on until a crop could be made.

Tenants, without a landlord to lean on, were thoroughly demoralized. Many of them were allowed to stay on in their houses and use a little land as best they could to raise some food to live on or to subsist on relief with the hope that they could hang on

until things got better. They could either do this or move to town
and join the ranks of the unemployed there. They had little
choice.

For a year or two the mad scramble in Washington to solve the
riddle was hectic. First there was the plow-up of a third of the
cotton acreage which had already been planted. This almost
caused a revolution, not only of the people but also of the mules.
A self-respecting mule who had been trained with many a curse
and lash to step carefully in the middle to avoid damage to the
tender plants just wouldn't change and walk on the row to plow
it up. Innocent little pigs were also slaughtered and their meat
doled out to keep their former owners from starving. Farmers
were getting a thorough shaking up from Hurried Harry Hopkins
and Hungry Henry Wallace and so no one was sure who was
dizziest.

After the first excitement the recovery programs settled down
to reasonably understandable economic objectives which were:
to raise farm incomes through acreage reduction and price sup-
ports, to conserve the soil, to keep as many people on the land
as possible until they could be absorbed by other sectors of the
economy, to alleviate the credit situation through government
loans, and to improve the level of living as much as possible
through home use production, rural electrification, and other
measures.

The New Deal alphabetical agencies inspired many pages of
ponderous economics and superheated political debate which
are now history. For the purposes of this volume, however, certain
relationships of the recovery measures to cotton farming and
especially to the Negro farmer are worth noting for their bearing
on the subsequent rapid changes in Southern agriculture.

I had had a close look at the Cotton Belt during the boll weevil
disorganization and I was now able to get two more looks in 1934
and 1937 when I, with assistants, surveyed hundreds of plantations
for the Works Progress Administration and made various field
trips as economic adviser for the Farm Security Administration.
The general picture was clear to me and to other observers
then close to the situation—namely that the recovery programs
had, at least temporarily, revitalized agriculture in the South. All
segments did not benefit equally but in general incomes were up,
debt burdens lightened, and home use production somewhat
stimulated. These financial benefits were, to some extent, re-

flected in better homes, more nourishing diets, and increasing interest in education.

The goal of curtailing production by reduction of acreage was, however, only partially successful. When the farmers were faced with the necessity of taking a substantial proportion of their cash crop acreage out of cultivation their enlightened self-interest impelled them to remove the least productive land and concentrate on the best acres, tilling them as intensively as possible; with the result that yields per acre shot up steeply and surpluses continued to mount, especially in 1937 when acreage control was completely removed.

Acreage reduction also made it difficult to hold as many families as desirable on the land until they could find opportunities elsewhere. It was elementary that fewer acres and more efficient cultivation spelled a sharp reduction in labor requirements. The more efficient tenants were kept under regular contract and the less efficient allowed to stay on rent free to live off odd jobs and a garden plot or to drift off as displaced men. In normal times this elimination of the inefficient producers from the labor force would have improved the health of agriculture like draining the puss from a boil, but this effort at readjustment came at a time when the whole economy was depressed and the displaced tenants only piled up relief burdens.

Diversification was the natural corollary to the reduction in the money crop. To many farmers this meant cattle. In the Deep South grass grows without encouragement and provides almost year round grazing with little pasture upkeep. All that was needed was a fence around the pasture, the introduction of a few head of stock and a little attention. Of course such natural pastures could be, and were, greatly improved by the application of lime and seeding with better grasses. Funds for this purpose were available from soil conservation benefits. Far less labor was required to tend cattle than had previously been used on these acres and the new enterprise absorbed only a small proportion of the displaced tenants.

Thus some of the recovery programs were definitely of the emergency stop-gap nature. They held an outmoded system of agriculture together and kept an excess supply of labor on the land. They were like patches on a leaky balloon, adequate for the moment but offering no guarantee against future leaks unless some of the pressure could be alleviated.

One of the most conspicuous advances in Southern farming of enduring value was registered in soil conservation by Hugh Bennett, of North Carolina. He had been an evangelist for the soil for many years but the do-nothing policies of the pre-New Deal Federal Government had confined his activities to research and exhortation. The positive programs of recovery opened the way to put his ideas into practice, with the result that more progress was made in conserving the soil in the 1930's than in the preceding 100 years. Experimentation and improved practices developed rapidly and many states passed acts authorizing the formation of soil conservation districts where the farmers of both races could democratically determine the best land use and receive aid from the Soil Conservation Service in saving their most valuable possession. These districts were so valuable to the farmer that, by 1957, they have increased to over twenty-five hundred in number and include most of the important farming areas of the nation. About one-third of them are located in the South.

In addition to soil conservation there was a modest program for taking out of agricultural use the submarginal lands which were too far exhausted to produce efficiently. Under this program nine million acres in the South were converted to forest, recreation areas, or other non-agricultural uses. Some of the former cultivators of this land were assisted in locating on other farms. Others joined the ranks of the displaced.

The extent to which the recovery program aided the landlord and the extent to which it benefited the tenant has been the subject of heated controversy. Since the total result was the sum of thousands of individual transactions the final answer to this question will probably never be known. The independent Negro owner probably fared as well as the white owner and the few cash renters were similarly situated. Under the law, however, the cropper was a dependent laborer, merely an interested third party in any arrangement between the landlord and the government. Thus the extent to which he shared in the recovery was partly dependent on the good graces of his landlord.

The landlord decided which land would be retired and how the remainder would be cultivated, whether by wage labor or by croppers; how the benefit check would be divided between cash for the tenant and credit on his past debts; how, and at what rate of interest, production credit loans were passed on to tenants. Under these circumstances, it was human nature for some landlords to chisel and for tenants who did not know all of the intricacies of their accounts to feel that they were shortchanged even when landlords had been fair. On balance it may be said that the owners profited substantially from the first few years of the recovery program and the tenants to a limited degree. The general effect of all these measures was to strengthen the managerial position and benefit labor only indirectly.

The visits of my assistants to about 250 plantations first in 1934 subsequently in 1937 have been summed up as follows:

Between 1934 and 1937 landlords enlarged their holdings somewhat. The yield of cotton increased from 268 pounds to 456 pounds per acre. The number of livestock showed a substantial growth; cows increased by more than 50 percent and pigs practically doubled. The resident families on plantations decreased by almost 10 percent. This decline in labor demand must be attributed largely to mechanization and other increases in efficiency. The use of tractors also increased. Landowners' mortgages had been reduced from $13,000 to $11,900 and their interest rates were less. In spite of government programs, production credit was still high, costing the landlord about 12 percent and the tenant as high as 36 percent.

Landlords' net cash incomes went up from $2,500 to $3,600. Considering the risk, and the managerial and production problems to be solved this would seem a small return for the effort. Tenants' money incomes were still less impressive, rising from $263 to $300 about two-thirds being collected in cash and one-third in subsistence advances. In addition, their home use production was estimated at about $100.

So much for the workings of the purely economic recovery programs. They were not enough. Throughout the previous discussion we have mentioned displaced tenants, men separated from agriculture altogether and not eligible for recovery benefits. For them there were, at first, only relief benefits. Later the farm security program was tailored to the needs of the families who could be reestablished on the land. More than a million rural families were aided in the South in 1938 through general relief and the Works Progress Administration and farm security programs. About 600,000 of these families included employable workers with some farm experience. Many ex-farmers were included among the families who applied for relief but could not be accepted because of lack of funds.

It did not make sense to clutter up the relief rolls with experienced farmers when land was available which they could use to become self-supporting. A program was needed for the man who had been entirely crowded off the farm. Accordingly the Farm Security Administration was authorized to make grants to those who had prospects for getting on their feet again. In about ten years of operation the program disbursed only about one-fifth of the amount spent by the Agricultural Adjustment Administration in the South and much of this was repaid as the loans were due.

Toward the close of its program the Farm Security Administration had removed thousands of farmers from the relief rolls in the South and helped them toward self-sufficiency and self respect. The Negro received a full share of these benefits.

After its early development by Harry Hopkins and Rex Tugwell, the guidance of the Farm Security Administration was assumed by Will W. Alexander, former director of the Commission on Interracial Cooperation. His intimate knowledge of the South enabled him to adapt the program to the needs of the South and the Negro and to leave a lasting imprint on the region.

The unique contribution of the Farm Security plan arose from its supervisory and educational activities. Most of the borrowers had been tenants, entirely dependent on a landlord for planning and supervision. In a sense Farm Security became a substitute for the landlord sending trained men and women to spread sound agricultural practices. The previous plans of the landlord had been based on making cash crop production a success. On the other hand the new program was designed to convert the tenant into a successful general farmer who would be able to pay his rent from the proceeds of the cash crop and also to provide a decent living for his family from vegetable and meat production.

Each loan was conditioned on the adoption of a farm plan which was carefully worked out by experts in agriculture and home economics, taking into account the land resources and family labor available and the amount of working capital needed to make it work. Women were enlisted in the planning of the family budget including the necessary canning and preservation of the family food. This was a novel and potent element in the success of family after family. The "precious" cooker became a central feature of family rehabilitation.

The step-by-step execution of the plan was also supervised by experts and the intangible educational benefits were undoubtedly as valuable as the cash advance. Additional assistance was given in debt adjustment and the encouragement of cooperative buying. As of 1938 the average net worth of over one hundred thousand Southern borrowers had been increased by nearly three-fourths since they had been under the guidance of the program. In the meantime the burden of supporting them in idleness was removed from the relief agencies.

In the later stages of the program particularly promising borrowers were placed on a land purchase program which granted long term loans to tenants who wished to become owners. Incidentally, when it was discovered that some of the borrowers who fell behind in their payments were forced to do so because of illness in the family, a medical program was organized in cooperation with county medical associations who agreed to care for these families and receive their fees from increases in the loans to cover this item.

Like any assistance to the Negro which is not controlled by the white land owners, Farm Security met with suspicion and some active opposition by the conservative element. Whispers of that devil word "communism" could occasionally be heard. On the whole, however, the effort was remarkably well received by the farm extension agents, merchants, and planters who had a chance to see it work. In fact, its policies were so outstandingly effective in aiding low-income farmers that they have been adopted as an essential feature of American programs for the assistance of other under-developed agricultural nations.

Other measures of lasting benefit to the South were launched by the Tennessee Valley Authority, the Rural Electrification Administration, and the Public Roads Administration. These provided cheap power for farm and industry, made current readily available in the farm home, and made it easier for the farmer to get to town. The conveniences of the city were brought to the farm. Few farms now have to collect wood for the stove or fuss with smoky kerosine lamps. Electric pumps bring water into the house and in many areas television aerials sprout from the lowliest roofs.

The expansion of industry during World War II and the postwar boom went a long way toward taking the pressure off the land. Movement from the farms which had been slowed by the depression picked up its former speed and between 1940 and 1950 both the white and Negro farm populations shrank by twenty-five percent, taking nearly four and a half million people off of Southern farms. There is every indication that this exodus continues, since the number of farm operators showed a further drop from 1950 to 1954.

This has meant that Dixie at last, has joined the rest of the nation in the trend to efficiency which has led the farmer to produce more on fewer acres and with less labor. The Southern farmer has shared in that phenomenal gain in labor productivity which is the envy of the rest of the world.

There has been an exodus of mules from the Cotton Belt as well as of people. Between 1950 and 1954 the number of horses and mules decreased by over half-million. Perhaps they couldn't stand the shame of being compelled to plow up growing cotton. The mules had been not only the cropper's work animal but also his method of getting to town. But this defection of the tenant farmer's traditional pal, the mule, was more than offset by the tripling of the number of trucks on Southern farms from 1930 to 1955 and the multiplication of the number of tractors by six times.

A few other figures from the agricultural census of 1954 indicate that the Southern farmer also is living much better. Telephones are in over a fourth of the homes and nearly 90 percent have electricity. About half have piped running water. More than a fourth have television set, almost as many have home freezers, and 15,000 boasted electric pig brooders. Fewer workers meant fewer houses and much of the substandard housing has been demolished, leaving a more cheerful landscape. Prosperity has come to those who could hang on in Southern agriculture partially because so many have gone elsewhere, removing the pressure of an excess labor supply and compelling the efficient use of the labor remaining.

Furthermore it is apparent that the shrinkage has sharply reduced the number of sharecroppers the South could well afford to do without.

Since 1930 the total decrease in tenants has exceeded a million. The drop in the number of Negro tenants accounts for 400,000 of this decline. Today the number of Negro tenants, especially croppers, is far less than half that in 1930.

All during the period there also has been a decrease in the number of farm laborers. The remaining laborers are better off and they no longer have to hang around for seasonal jobs. Most are

closer to steady employment since many are now truck drivers and
tractor and combine operators with much more know-how than
formerly and with proportionately higher wages.

As of 1957, the Cotton South is only partially mechanized. Less
than half the farms have tractors. The system is still in transition.
Some plantations still operate mostly with mules and sharecroppers. They may have one or two tractors for special jobs. Others
are heavily dependent on tractors. These have, for the most part,
tended to replace croppers with tractor drivers or wage hands.
Some croppers remain as a supply of seasonal labor. In these cases
new sharing arrangements have been worked out. The production
of smaller and less costly tractors and combines has made it possible for the family-sized farm as well as the plantation to reap
the benefits of mechanical efficiency allowing the increase in acres
harvested and the reduction in drudgery.

A close second to the coming of the tractor as the mainspring
of farm progress has been the revolution in marketing. Farmers
with extra eggs, vegetables or fruit, or farmers' wives with cakes
and preserves, have only to take them to the nearest farmers'
market. Or if his perishables are produced on a larger scale, one
of the many frozen food companies may take them off his hands.
The freezer locker has replaced the smokehouse for preserving
meat. While the tractor has made it possible to produce cotton
with less labor, improved marketing practices have made it possible to supplant cotton as the chief cash crop. The spread of
growing cities and small towns provide a market for anything that
the Southern farmer can grow.

In summary: large-scale plantations with centrally controlled
holdings remain characteristic of the Lower South but they require
more capital and less labor. They are more productive and the
general level of rural living is vastly improved.

CHAPTER 7

Restless People

A popular cotton belt story concerned a down at the heels sharecropper who was standing by a ferry trying to beg a dime to get across. A farmer he approached asked him whether he had a job or any friends on the other side. He said no but that he thought things just might be better over there. That was the frame of mind of the whole area—always groping for something better. I discovered that nearly half of the Negro families of Athens were not born there but had lately moved in from surrounding farms. Had I put the same question to the heads of white families I would probably have found that as many of them had left neighboring cotton patches to work in the cotton mills. Town wages were just enough higher than farm wages to be a real inducement.

As of 1910, about two-thirds of the tenants in Georgia, white and colored, had lived on their farms a year or less; only one in twenty had lived in the same house more than ten years. Anyone travelling the country roads after the harvest would pass dozens of families on the move—a bony mule pulling a rickety wagon (usually borrowed). All of their worldly possessions consisted of of little more than an old bed, some broken springs, some straw mattresses, one or two crude chairs, and a few battered cooking utensils. There were usually several children perched on top and an equal number of hounds plodding alongside.

The Plantation Belt was a land of semi-nomads. They did not stay in one place long enough to make friends or form community ties. Small wonder they had no interest in improving the land which they cultivated or the house in which they lived. If they had a roof to keep them dry and walls to temper the wind, they made no effort to patch the floor of the porch or brace up the sagging steps. To make such improvements would no more have occurred to them than it would occur to a city tenant to decorate an apartment rented for a year.

Church memberships were constantly changing, the buildings were in poor repair and the treasury perpetually in debt. Rural preachers, to hold body and soul together, had to serve two or three churches, preaching only once or twice a month at each one. Often enough they had to supplement this income by working as tenant farmers or laborers. Rural teachers hardly had time to become acquainted with pupils before they moved on, regardless of whether it was in the middle of the school term or not. There was almost a total lack of community life.

The movements were varied but at first were mostly from farm to farm. Some families moved from the farm to the nearby village and others into small cities. The net movement was away from the Black Belt and into newer cotton areas.

A vague discontent with the sharecropping system was the chief drive behind the restlessness, but there was also a steady pressure generated by the rapid growth of population in a land where agriculture was declining. In 1910, four out of every five Southern families lived in rural areas and were far more successful in raising children than they were in raising crops.

Half-grown children were an economic asset to tenant farmers since the landlord allocated land to his tenants in accordance with their ability to cultivate it. One man alone could not hope for more than a one-mule crop, but if he had one or two sturdy children to help in the field at chopping and picking time he was eligible for a two-mule allotment.

As a result the Cotton Belt was bearing the expense of rearing a larger proportion of children than other sections. Here the pioneer pattern which, two generations before had produced large families all over the nation, persisted into the twentieth century. While the South had a third of its population of school age, the industrial sections had less than one-fourth.

Since the agriculture of the region was barely supporting the existing population, the excess youth as they matured were compelled to move. In other words the plantations up to 1930, had exported a fourth of their natural increase and still managed to gain slightly in spite of this migration. About one out of each eight children born in the South at the time was destined to make his contribution to the development of some other region.

Even at the low cost of living of those days I estimated that the region had by 1930 spent from $5 to $10 billion dollars in rearing children who contributed to the upbuilding of other states. Their repayment, as far as could be determined, was an occasional kick in the pants for not rearing them to suit the tastes of their future employers.

Poor farmers were not the only ones who left. Some of the more ambitious youth had to seek opportunity to develop in other sections. Two of my classmates who have probably gone farthest in life, one the head of a large publishing house and another a corporation executive who became a cabinet member, had to move North to find opportunity for the full use of their talents. All in all, this constituted a marked drain of ablest youth from the region. In an analysis of eminent men of science and letters whose names were listed in *Who's Who* and *American Men of Science* it appeared that in 1930, forty-five percent of the eminent social scientists and sixty percent of the natural scientists who were born in the South were living elsewhere. This drain is difficult to measure except at the top but it doubtless extends down the educational scale depriving the region of the contribution of some of its most able and most energetic sons.

In 1916 the movement of farm population took on a dramatic new importance. The boll weevil had arrived in Georgia and this tiny insect created a deeper depression in the Cotton Belt than the so-called great depression of 1930. Cotton yields were reduced to an average of less than a third of a bale per acre. On many farms they were wiped out. Some planters lost their land to the banks and others let their tenants go rather than risk advancing them money to produce a crop which might never mature.

The Negro looked on the boll weevil as a supernatural visitation, something akin to the plagues which were called down on the ancient Egyptians. Preachers warned their congregations not to fight the pest because it was sent by God and therefore had some sort of divine status. It took a great deal of tact and patience to overcome this superstition. A planter called his people together one morning and explained that the weevil laid an egg in the cotton bud, causing it to turn yellow when the grub ate the inside. The best way to control the pest which had been discovered up to that time was to gather these yellow buds and burn them. When he explained this to his tenants and urged them to start picking off the yellow buds, one old sister chirped: "No sir, those bugs were sent by God and the preacher said it would be a sin to kill them". The planter thought a while and then said, "Well auntie, I guess everything on earth was sent by God. Suppose your head was full of nits and lice, would you do anything about that?" That was all that was necessary to decide the issue.

The whole plantation belt was so demoralized by the weevil

that the situation was of grave concern to the United States Department of Labor and, as a result, I was asked to make some first hand observations. I found the landlords almost as panicky as tenants. Those who were in debt were in fear of foreclosure; those not in debt were puzzled as to whether they should gamble on an uncertain crop or a labor force that might evaporate after piling up debts. As in the previous 30 years, Negroes also were moving from areas not yet reached by the boll weevil, but the dislocation in the areas of heaviest weevil damage was the most intense.

In these demoralized areas labor agents from Northern industries which were beginning to expand under the stimulus of World War I came to recruit the Negroes by the hundreds. Word would spread that on a certain day a special car would leave for Detroit or Chicago or Buffalo and on the appointed day a flock would gather at the railroad station for a free journey to the promised land. Sometimes the cars would be there, but at other times the report would prove to be false. The reaction of the planters was immediate. The very people who before had been the loudest in advocating the deportation of all Negroes, were the first ones to fight against these raids by labor agents. Some counties passed laws requiring labor agents to pay licenses fees as high as $1,000. In other cases such agents were simply shooed out of town before they could make any offers. As in the past, many Southerners would insist that they would be better off if the Negroes were somewhere else, but let them start somewhere else in numbers which would reduce the labor supply, and howls of protest would go up.

Some sections made efforts to get away from cotton and grow other crops. A county in South Alabama which tried cattle was so pleased with the experiment that a monument to the boll weevil was erected in gratitude for getting rid of King Cotton. These efforts were short-lived. Some degree of control was obtained over the boll weevil and World War I brought high prices for cotton. As a result the Plantation South went back to cotton culture in a big way. A few years after the boll weevil monument was erected the Alabama county again raised more cotton than ever.

Cotton or no cotton, the movement continued. Negroes who had come to the city wrote back to their friends giving them glowing accounts of city life and these friends infected others. Preachers moved and whole congregations followed. For the first time the Negro tenant began to exercise his only really effective protest against plantation conditions, which was to move away from them.

Economic conditions were not the only cause of Negro unrest. A rebellion against brutality from which there was no redress caused many to seek the shelter of the city. In counties where lynchings had occurred planters were unanimous in testifying that their labor force was seriously disorganized and many were uprooted from the land.

The city Negro was free from the haunting fear of violence even though he might be handled in a summary fashion by the city police and courts. As poor as were the city schools they were better than the rural makeshifts. The city offered an escape from the drab poverty of life on the farm.

At first the chief destination of the uprooted croppers was Southern cities, as late as 1910 less than half million Southern born Negroes were living elsewhere. With such plentiful supply of labor pressing into town, the cities became low wage areas. For jobs which could be taken over by countrymen with little training the wage spread between farm and city was slight. In highly skilled jobs it was greater. In skilled occupations, however, the Negro was subjected to intense competition from white migrants who were just as anxious to leave the plantation as they were and who were willing to ignore the fact that certain occupations had been traditionally reserved to Negroes. The take-over of these jobs was facilitated by the appearance in the South of all-white unions which choked off the flow of Negro apprentices.

Some earlier students thought that the depressed conditions in the South indicated that about a third of the people should move elsewhere. But the area as a whole was not overpopulated; there were simply too many people on the farms. The population has doubled since 1900 and in spite of this increase in numbers the level of living has risen. This has come about largely because of a redistribution of population between the farms and the cities within the South.

Getting underway slowly after the Civil War, the depopulation of the farms was speeded up first by the disorganization of the boll weevil and World War I industrial expansion and again by the demands for industrial manpower in World War II and subsequent boom years. The movement has continued down to the present date. Discontent with rural life has been the main driving force and city jobs the main attractive force, but there are times, notably during the depression years, when the cityward movement continued in spite of the lack of job opportunities. In 1950, two-thirds of the nation's 15 million Negroes lived in the South. But, whereas the Southern Negroes in 1900 were eighty percent farm dwellers, by 1950, they were seventy percent in the cities and villages.

The natural increase of the white population has been greater than that of the Negro and a higher proportion of Negroes have moved to other regions with the result that the South as a whole and each of the Southern States has become whiter.

As the rural population pressure lessened the glut of workers was reduced. No longer could the farms count on an oversupply of labor which could be used wastefully. No longer were the cities full of workers who would take almost any job on any terms. As the wages of men increased, more and more women could stay home with the children and fewer and fewer were willing to accept domestic service at low wages.

The Negro business and professional groups expanded and a few more industrial opportunities were opened. Numerous national firms, taking advantages of the plentiful Southern labor supply and the inducements offered by the Southern States, opened branch plants in the South and some of them employed substantial numbers of colored workers.

The occupational shifts have raised the level of incomes of Negroes substantially. Southern city Negroes now earn about three-fourths as much as Negroes in the North—but only about half of what white workers earn in the same cities.

With increased incomes the more substantial element of the Negroes began to demand and get better houses. Neater blocks began to appear in onetime slum areas and more well-kept automobiles were parked along the curb. Both the Negro and the white man took note of this new economic power. The Negro who had formerly been in the market only for staple foods and work clothes, became the prospect for real estate and automobiles and the customer of department and chain stores. It was this newly developed economic power which recently enabled the Negroes of Montgomery, Alabama, and Tallahassee, Florida, to bring bus companies to the verge of bankruptcy simply by withholding their fares. The first instances of the organized use of economic power by the city Negro, these boycotts were accompanied by a spate of prospective and rumored action of a similar sort. Negroes threatened to boycott some merchants because it was reported they were supporting the White Citizens Councils. On the other hand, white people threatened to boycott a particular brand of beer because the brewing company had bought a membership in the NAACP for its Negro salesmen. Some white people threatened to boycott Ford cars because of the supposed responsibility of the Ford Foundation for stirring up Negro unrest. This was so prevalent that it was duly recorded and commented on by the *Wall Street Journal.*

Interesting possibilities are opened up as to future use of the boycott technique and its repercussons on race relations. The white business men are in the middle when excitement runs high in a controversy of this kind. They as well as the Negro have discovered that dollars are neither white nor black but green.

On the whole, over a period of time, the wholesale shift of the Negro population has made some improvement in race relations. The South has become accustomed to the presence of the city Negro, who is a far more sophisticated fellow than the common laborer or sharecropper of two generations ago. This is not to imply that the progress was phenomenal. New arrivals from the country continued to bring their country ways into the city. They were willing to live in houses little better than the shack they had left behind. Low wages forced them to accept what they could pay for. As a result the undesirable sections were filled to capacity with cheap frame houses each crowded to the limit. Those who were incapable of adjusting to city ways fell into poverty or petty crime. In contrast with the sections where the ambitious, thrifty Negroes lived there were areas of crime and disease which were the problem areas for the police, the social workers, and the sanitary workers. There are still slums, but not such slummy slums as before. Fewer houses are without water and sanitary facilities. More streets are improved and more paint has been spread in some sections. The great mass of Negroes, however, are advancing so gradually that their white neighbors are hardly aware of what is happening. As gradual as it has been, this progress is enough to outdate previous stereotypes of the race.

Race relations in the rural Black Belts have also benefited from the shifting of population. In 1900 there were over 300 counties in which more than half of the population was Negro and in many of these the ratio was more than three to one. These are the hard core areas where plantation life dominates community relations, where the whites are in contact mainly with ignorant tenants, where outside ideas are slowest to penetrate, and where the Old-South pattern of race relations is most persistent. By 1950 the number of such counties had been cut in half. For a half-century the white population of every Southern state had increased more than the Negroes and from 1940 to 1950 six Southern states had actual losses in Negro population. The problem areas are not only shrinking in size but becoming whiter in complexion. The talk of Negro domination is less frequent, nor do we hear so much of the necessity of keeping the Negro in his place.

The outlook on race relations has also been broadened by migration into the region from other areas. Industrialization and broader markets have attracted a steady stream of settlers. Several million who now reside in the South were born elsewhere and have ideas of race based on experience in other sections. Likewise hundreds of thousands of boys have returned from the armed forces after service in other lands where customs are different. All in all the cities of the New South are becoming more cosmopolitan. A respectable number have actually begun to vote Republican.

Thus the redistribution of population is at the root of a revolution in race relations. It has substituted city Negroes for country Negroes, changed race contacts, reduced the number of problem areas, and exerted a healthy influence on all phases of race relations.

It is to be expected that normal migration will continue to reduce the proportion of Negroes in the old plantation areas but this will be a slow process, since it requires a fairly heavy movement just to drain off the natural increase and keep the farm population stationary. Aside from the reluctance of many Negroes to move, migration is an expensive process and there is some question as to how fast the expansion of industry can profitably absorb larger numbers. Besides Negroes are practically indispensable to Southern agriculture. If, by some miracle, they should disappear suddenly from the region, the depression would be greater than anything which it has ever seen.

CHAPTER 8

Segregation Northern Style

The movement of Negroes to the North was hardly a trickle before the boll weevil made its unwelcome appearance.

In 1910 less than half a million Southern-born Negroes lived in the North. This was partially because of the proximity of small towns and cities in the South and partially because of lack of opportunity in other regions. Up to that time a constant flood of European immigrants had amply supplied the demands for industrial labor. During the first part of the twentieth century some years saw net immigration from Europe of over a million. This flood was dried up by the outbreak of war in Europe in 1914. After World War I there were a few years of renewed immigration but in 1924 Congress limited the intake to 150,000 per year.

A mass movement requires both a push from the old area and a pull to the new. As long as foreigners were plentiful in industrial areas there was no pull on the Southern population, but the stoppage of immigration came at a time when the boll weevil was exerting a compelling push from the South, and the expanding war industries were creating a vaccum in the Northern labor market. It was this that started the first real exodus of the Negro to industry.

The first time I had a close-up view of the pull of Northern industry was in 1914, when the Ford Motor Company announced that it was raising wages for common labor to $5 a day for 8 hours of work. This unprecedented news traveled through the South like a prairie fire at a time when day labor there was getting 75 cents to 85 cents a day,

At first it was the white boys who got most excited about earning $5 a day in Detroit. A young fellow who had not amounted to much in his home town would disappear and after a few months show up again in a silk shirt and fancy clothes, eager to boast of his venture in the North. For awhile Negroes did not pay too much attention to this, they had the feeling that the opportunities were solely for white men.

It was not long before the personnel managers of big corporations began to realize that there was an ample supply of Negro laborers eager to get the hot and heavy industrial jobs formerly filled by the Russian, Polish, Hungarian and Italian immigrants. As a result, from 1910 to 1930 the number of Southern-born Negroes in the North increased by 1,500,000. There were still, however, 3,000,000 Negroes living in Southern cities as against slightly more than 2,000,000 in Northern cities.

The sharecroppers, white and colored, came out of the South with the high hopes of the children of Isarel coming out of Egypt. But if this scriptural parallel may be continued it will be recalled the land of milk and honey turned out to be pretty tough going for the Israelites for quite a long time.

The new invasion swelled the Negro city population rapidly. New York increased over sixty thousand from 1910 to 1920 filling up the established 59th Street neighborhood and the settlement on the present site of the Pennsylvania station. Harlem was soon taken over as a Negro area and rapidly became the largest Negro city in the world. The settlements in Chicago and Philadelphia ballooned with equal speed. In addition, new footholds were established in some of the booming Midwestern industrial areas. The Negro population of Detroit increased six-fold. Cleveland tripled, Chicago more than doubled, and Pittsburgh, Akron, and Gary acquired some of the new labor. The concentration and speed of the movement was unforeseen and the cities were totally unprepared for the new problems which the Southern peasants brought with them.

Although some of these cities were accustomed to the presence of a small number of Negroes the newcomers were radically different. Less accustomed to city ways, they were cruder, noiser, less orderly. Their coming dismayed the white people and irritated the established colored families who felt that their status was being jeopardized by interlopers. The red carpet of welcome was not spread by the white people or even by the people of their own race.

The first industries to hire Negro labor were those which required large numbers of unskilled workers in jobs that were becoming undesirable to the foreigners who had begun to move up to better jobs. These were the meat packing and automobile, rubber, and steel industries. Others showed a marked hesitancy in experimenting with this new type of worker. Some were afraid that they would not be accepted as fellow workers by white employees. Some welcomed Negroes in unskilled jobs but offered little hope of advancement.

The initial narrow opportunities for Negro workers were expanded somewhat during the labor shortages in World War I and the recovery of the 1920's but they were still spotty. I learned that in the North in 1929 about 17 percent of the concerns employed Negroes only as janitors and porters and that of the remainder 44 percent employed Negroes solely in unskilled operations.

Progress in the manufacturing occupations was greatly hampered by the policies of organized labor. The Congress of Industrial Organizations had not yet appeared on the scene and although the American Federation of Labor, in its resolutions, favored no racial discrimination and paid lip service to the organization of Negroes, the decision really rested with the international and local unions. At that time 24 of the internationals excluded Negroes by constitutional clauses or ritual. As late as 1929 a canvass of Negro membership in trade unions revealed only 61,000 Negro members in mixed unions or less than 2 percent of the total union membership. It was crystal clear that as much as the Negro was needed by some employers, he was not welcomed with open arms by his white fellow workers.

Thus in the few years between the first great rush to the North and the onset of the depression the Negro succeeded in getting only a slight entering wedge into organized labor and had barely begun to ascend the scale of skill. The great depression canceled most of this gain. When the skies fell in 1929 the newcomers had the least seniority. They were the last hired and first fired and their unemployment rates were highest. In all the North, in 1930, fourteen per cent of the Negro males were unemployed as against eight per cent of the white males. In the newer industrial centers the situation was much worse. Detroit reported that one-third of the white males were jobless and almost two-thirds of the Negro males. In Cleveland the rates were almost as staggering.

Few, however, returned to the South as unemployment was building up there also and, besides, being "on the welfare" was more comfortable in the North than in the South. In fact, there is some indication that unemployment did not completely discourage the movement North and that a trickle continued.

Heavy unemployment persisted through the depression years

and into the defense period. It was not until intense manpower shortages again began to develop in World War II that the excess Negro workers were absorbed. During the early 1940's we had a spectacle of developing labor shortages alongside of excessive Negro unemployment and it required special pressure from the manpower agencies to overcome reluctance to rehire Negroes.

Residential segregation was as rigid in the North as it was in the South if not even more so. Just as the Negro moved into the less desirable jobs formerly held by foreigners so they moved into less desirable houses which had formerly been occupied by the unskilled white workers. They took accommodations which white landlords found it more profitable to rent to them than to white people. These were usually in run-down neighborhoods where dwellings were very old and in sad state of disrepair. They were usually in blighted areas which were in transition from residence to business. Under these circumstances the owners were willing to rent property for a few years for temporary income, but not willing to make any improvements or repairs.

In most cases the land in these areas had already been over-crowded with buildings and the high rents, low incomes, and lax living standards led to further overcrowding in the houses. Dwellings, originally intended for one family, were often occupied by two and three migrant families, sometimes with lodgers, all sharing the same bath. This built up some unbelievable densities. The density of Negro residence areas, in most Northern cities was soon well over twice that of the white areas—in some cities four times. Some blocks in New York and Chicago became the densest areas in the world.

Thus an explosive pressure for expansion accumulated. In many cases, however, expansion in some directions was blocked by adjoining manufacturing or commercial areas and in other directions by hostile white communities. In the early stages of transition from white to Negro occupancy, property values dropped sharply. Many owners panicked and sold out at a sacrifice. Efforts to choke off the spread of Negro neighborhoods took on a variety of forms ranging from propaganda to raw violence. Pledges by members of real estate dealer's associations not to sell or rent to Negroes and covenants written into deeds which restricted the future sale of the property to white owners were the most usual practices.

When these were ineffective, vandalism, arson, and bombing were the deterrents used—frequently and unabashedly—to discourage movement from the Black Belts. Latent racial antagonism was brought into the open and tension and bitterness hung like a pall over the disputed neighborhoods. Numerous race riots South and North marked the year 1919. Those in the North, including the bloody outbreak in Chicago, grew out of the friction engendered by the expansion of Negro neighborhoods. Since the process of expansion was continuous, violence did not disappear after the initial rush. In a little over two years in the 1940's forty-six terrorist attacks against homes occupied by Negroes in Chicago were recorded, one being the case of a home which was completely dismantled by neighbors.

As one of the fastest growing cities, Detroit also has been the scene of continuous friction. Violence in 1942 was recorded by Robert C. Weaver as follows: "On February 28, 1942, 12 Negro families attempted to move into the Sojourner Truth war housing project. They were met by several hundred whites two blocks from the site. Local officials immediately conferred with the police and were informed that the latter could not offer protection to the would-be tenants. Rioting started. The police took no steps to protect the Negroes; as a result, of the 100 arrests only three were white; of the 38 persons hopitalized, all but 5 were colored." It required the protection of the militia to secure some of these homes for Negro war workers. This, however, was only a curtain raiser for the riot of 1943 in which there were 35 deaths and 500 injured—apart from several million dollars in property damage and a million man hours lost in war production.

Singling out Chicago and Detroit does not mean that they had a monopoly on lawlessness. At one time or another in the past 20 years, most Northern cities which had a considerable influx of Negroes have experienced friction. As in the South, the police were slow to arrest the white people involved. These incidents bred bitterness on both sides and kept cities in a state of tension. They recalled Mr. Dooley's wisecrack to the affect that sometimes he thought the Negro was better off in the hands of his Southern oppressors than in those of his Northern liberators.

Unfortunately about the time when the available Negro areas had been filled beyond their capacity our entry into World War I brought all new construction to a standstill and sped up the move-

ment still more. (The same situation marked the outbreak of
World War II.)

Expanded demand for the limited supply of housing raised rents
to artificial levels. This pyramiding demand and restricted supply
was a perfect situation for the real estate operator. Numerous
housing surveys of Northern cities in recent years, including one
of my own, have, without exception, revealed higher rents paid
by Negroes than by white people for similar accommodations. In
my inquiry I found that in 1920 in Gary, Indiana, where the
quality of housing for Negroes was greatly inferior to that for
whites, the average rent per room was $4 for whites and $5.64 for
Negroes. In Buffalo, rents for comparable dwellings ranged from
four times as much for Negroes in the cheapest quarters to 25 percent higher in the more expensive. So it went in varying degrees
in all the cities which I surveyed. The method of reaping this
richer harvest from Negro tenants usually involved splitting up
of old houses or apartments into smaller units without an off-
setting reduction in rent.

The only way in which the low income Negro families could
pay these rents was by doubling up or taking in lodgers. This
process compounded overcrowding, multiplied fire hazards and
other building code violations, and encouraged unspeakable sanitary conditions.

Here we have a perfect formula for slum building: Move excessive numbers of people, who have had low standards of living
and become accustomed to exploitation, into already run-down
neighborhoods with substandard housing. Jack up the rents so
house crowding is intensified. Put a tight fence around them so
that subsequent arrivals can only pile up and aggravate conditions.
Neglect recreation facilities. Throw in some slackness of city officials in enforcing health and sanitation safeguards, and negligence
of the police in maintaining law and order, and the resulting
mess is inevitable. Given these large and solid Negro neighborhoods, school segregation became a matter of geography without
necessity of law, and all community facilities became separate
and unequal.

It will be noted that this process went forward without any
legal compulsion. Settlements chosen by the Negroes first because
they wanted to associate with their own people and because the
rents were within their means later, especially in the North, were

crystallized by white reluctance to associate with Negroes, or to see their property deteriorate, and cemented in place by community pressures and extra-legal violence. In fact, there is no law either in the South or the North that Negroes must live in particular places. The cheap rent sections of the city were the iron bed of Procrustes into which the Negro migrant had to fit himself as best he could.

The politician was another element of the Northern city that welcomed segregated Negro communities. Such a large bloc of votes, unified by race consciousness, was too tempting to be overlooked. The Negro began to flex his political muscles and in some cities assumed the balance of power between the parties. Certain of these cities held the key to the majority in states with large electoral votes, giving the Negro bargaining power and national recognition. Solidification of the Negro vote in definite wards and even larger areas made it possible to elect Negroes to city offices, to secure for them political appointments, and finally to elect representatives in the national Congress.

As in the South, the segregated community fostered the development of separate businesses and professions. Growing congregations came to the Negro preachers. Separate schools made jobs for Negro teachers. Negro stores had customers right at hand and they, in turn made jobs for Negro clerks. Harlem actually has a firm of Negro stockbrokers. The Negro community grew up as a cross section of the general community and a class of business and professional Negroes emerged who had a vested interest in segregation. They were of a divided mind about the process. Segregation made their advance possible, but even though they made better incomes, they wished to move to better neighborhoods. They aspired to better things than dirt and tenements. They wished to follow the footsteps recently trod by the foreign born who, as they learned American ways and acquired the means, were able to move out into better surroundings and give their children more advantages and prove that America is truly a land of opportunity. In a way it can be said that they wished to dissociate themselves from their own people.

As long as they wore the badge of color, however, they had a handicap which the foreigner lost when he lost his accent. The community at large resisted their efforts to get out of their straight jacket and the Ghettos persisted. These neighborhoods are slums in which the Negro becomes enmeshed and finds it well-nigh impossible to leave except by moving into another well defined Negro neighborhood and they have resisted all efforts at dissolution and are the earmarks of the principal Northern cities well into the second half of this century.

Robert C. Weaver, the Negro expert who has probably given this phenomenon closer study than any one else, concludes that the boom of the 1920's encouraged slum development and that the 1940's found the Negro in the Northern city as segregated as in the 1920's, if not more so. In spite of these handicaps, superior economic opportunity and legal protection continued to attract new migrants. From a negligible number in 1900, the Negro population of Northern cities had, by 1950, grown to over five million or a third of the Negroes of the nation.

In the days of the first rush to the cities, the Northerner was learning that in spite of all of his previous holier-than-thou protestations, he was, after all, pretty much a brother under the skin to the Southerner. The migrant fresh from the plantation was learning that he was no more loved in the North than in the South and was almost as easy a prey to exploitation in one place as in another until he began to protect himself with the ballot and made substantial economic progress.

Through all the vicissitudes of becoming a city dweller the Negro has been greatly helped by the Urban League, the National Association for the Advancement of Colored People and of late years, by the public housing authorities.

The Urban League was founded in 1910 as an interracial organization designed to assist in the adjustment of the Northern migrant. It soon spread to Southern cities and now has about fifty local organizations on both sides of the Mason and Dixon Line, supported in part, in most cities, by the community chest.

The League concentrated first on expanding Negro job opportunities—selling the white employers on the idea of using Negro labor. Notable success along this line led to the attack on a broad range of community problems, particularly housing. It has led movements to secure playgrounds, schools, and other public facilities; it has also operated day nurseries, baby clinics, child placement agencies, and numerous other services. It is a practical organization, attacking problems as they appear. Like all such cooperative organizations, it frequently comes under the fire from the "all or nothing" Negro leaders who contend it is too conciliatory of local sentiment and not sweeping enough in its objectives or militant enough in promoting them. However, the Urban League has won respect and solid backing in many cities.

The struggle of the Negro to achieve better living conditions in industrial cities has also required legislation and litigation. The brunt of the legal battle has been carried by the National Association for the Advancement of Colored People in its militant stand against discrimination in public housing and covenants restricting the use of private housing. This organization, together with the National Committee Against Discrimination in Housing did much to change housing policies of federal, state, and local governments and private property holders.

Public housing projects—two-thirds of which were initially planned for Negro occupancy—have provided badly needed additional space. In addition to the all-Negro projects, open occupancy policies recently adopted in a number of cities have scattered a few Negro families in all white neighborhoods.

Similar possibilities may develop from urban renewal projects. These schemes, however, involve tearing down existing substandard houses. Unless therefore an adequate supply of shelter is available to the displaced families elsewhere, such slum clearance can only cause overcrowding in other parts of the city.

The problem of the production of a sufficient number of houses whose rentals will be within the reach of low and middle income families in our cities is so vast that public housing projects cannot make a sufficient dent in it. New construction and changes in occupancy of private housing must eventually be depended upon if slum conditions are ameliorated.

The private housing situation for Negroes is also improving. Here and there private builders are building houses within a price range which can be afforded by the middle and upper income Negro families. Each family which moves from rented quarters into one of these newly purchased homes takes that much pressure off the crowded rental neighborhoods. The largest volume of middle-class housing which has been made available to Negroes has been in formerly white neighborhoods vacated by families that have joined the exodus to the suburbs. An increasing number of landlords whose buildings have been vacated by suburbanites have been renting to Negroes rather than carry a vacancy.

A stiff barrier, which formerly slowed the scattering of Negroes into new neighborhoods or the expansion of old neighborhoods, was removed in 1948 when the Supreme Court outlawed the covenants in deeds that limited future occupancy to white families. Along with this there has seemingly developed a greater tolerance on the part of lower and middle income white people to the presence of Negro families in their neighborhood.

The most substantial evidence of housing improvement is the increase in home ownership. Only 20% of the Negro city dwellers owned their house in 1940 but, by 1950 some 33% occupied their own property. The proportion of homeowners is even higher in the villages.

The number of decent houses into which the city Negro can move has expanded considerably and increasing numbers of families who are ambitious to escape the Ghetto can do so. All of this, however, has not been enough to rid the cities completely of their slums. For each hundred families which move out an almost equal number of families fresh from the country move in. As long as dissatisfaction with Southern conditions continues, and as long as jobs are plentiful in industrial areas, the cities will continue to grow and the migrants will occupy the run-down houses. To make any measurable progress, housing space available for non-whites must expand at a faster rate than population.

The production of an adequate number of houses for low and middle income groups is primarily an economic problem which has hardly begun to be solved. If, however, any substantial groups are barred artificially from access to large areas, the problem is complicated by the inability to match supply and demand effectively. Under these circumstances social problems are piled on top of economic problems. In addition to group purchasing power, customary habits, and attitudes enter the picture.

The ultimate objective of Negro leaders in the field of housing is the elimination of racial barriers as far as possible, and the creation of a situation in which the Negro, like his foreign born predecessor in the slums, can move into any house which he can afford on an unsegregated basis and, having moved, will be accepted casually as would be the case with any other neighbor.

It is apparent that considerable progress is under way in the provision of an adequate number of dwellings for the present urban Negro population but continued migration perpetuates the sub-standard housing areas. On the other hand the goal of casual acceptance as a neighbor is far from realization on a large scale. As long as the whites are not color blind and harbor resentment at the intrusion of Negroes and until the masses of Negroes can overcome some of the handicaps to which white people object, the extension of Negro occupancy in some places will create friction and ill will. The majority of Negroes have not yet had the full generation of equal economic opportunity and educational advantage which is essential for the elimination of differences that place a strain on good neighborliness.

CHAPTER 9

The High Price of Poverty

The foothold which the Negro had been able to secure in industry in the late 1920's was precarious at best, but his position was not so low that it could not sink lower before it began to rise. As the depression of the early 1930's deepened more and more workers suffered a complete loss of income, exhaustion of savings, and hopeless piling up of debt. Unemployment rose steadily upward from 3 million to 15 million.

These were days when desperate measures were seriously considered. One callous proposal was that restaurants and public eating places be exhorted to save what diners left on their plates for collection and distribution to the destitute. The scheme was spelled out: "Sanitary containers of five gallons each should be secured in large kitchens where restaurants are serving a volume business. The containers should be labeled 'Meat, Potatoes, Bread, and Other Items.' Some one from the Salvation Army with a truck should pick up the loaded containers every morning and leave the empty ones. When a man finishes his meal he should not leave ashes on the food which he was unable to consume. A card should be placed in each restaurant to read as follows, 'We will utilize all surplus wholesome food which is not consumed for the benefit of charity.' " This was only one of many suggestions made by well-meaning people who were blind to the obvious need for large-scale assistance from the Federal Government.

Meanwhile misery mounted. The Communist bogey was increasingly raised. But there were thousands of people who were genuinely concerned with the tragedy of unemployment and were willing to encourage anybody who might conceivably be of help in a desperate situation; these were easy prey for the Communist front organizations.

I passed through cities where the outside weatherboarding had been ripped off houses as high as a man could reach in the desperate effort to get fuel. Hoboes, too numerous to be coped with by trainmen, rode the tops of freight trains as thick as starlings on a telephone wire. There was no segregation on this transportation. Fortunate was the young man whose parents had held on to the family farm. He at least could go home and eat. Before anything could be done for these people two hurdles had to be overcome in the conservative mind. One was the conviction that the Federal Government never had been (hence never should be) concerned with the relief of poverty and the other was that the jobless were suffering not because of the breakdown of the economy but because of some personal inadequacy. They were said either never to have worked hard enough or never to have been thrifty enough to be worthy of consideration. In addition, it was alleged that the use of the nation's credit for this purpose would cause decline in the value of Government bonds which were furnishing a safe shelter for some of the wealth which had been salvaged from the wreckage.

In the early days of the New Deal I joined the stream of professors who were trooping to Washington from the colleges to indulge in the fascinating job of helping to chart the way for the Federal Government into the hitherto unexplored waters of the relief and prevention of poverty.

We were not always too sure of where we were going and there were many false starts but there was at least a sense of eagerness to get somewhere and a refusal to be discouraged by failure. Failures only sped greater effort. One had to be agile to keep up with the alphabet. In a little over five years I had some connection with CWA, FERA, RR, WPA, NYA, and two different agencies with the initials FSA. I missed out on PWA and CCC, and dozens of others not so directly concerned with unemployment.

The early New Deal programs were distinctly emergency stopgap measures, efforts to deal swiftly with an urgent need. One of the basic principles which became the guide for later programs was that there is no real substitute for a job. To maintain his self-respect a man needs work almost as much as he needs food to maintain his body. Work relief and public works, therefore— even though more costly—were the chief measures relied on to supply income up to the time when the revived economy could furnish jobs for those able to work.

But there were broad segments of the population which had no hope of securing access to normal employment. These were the aged, the blind, the temporarily disabled and dependent children. Harry Hopkins summed up this aspect of the problem in these words:

"The administration of relief and the researches we have made into the standards of living of the American family have uncovered for the public gaze a volume of chronic poverty unsuspected except by a few students and by those who have always experienced it. We might well ask where these people have been all our lives, if we did not already know the answer. The poorest have in large numbers been kept alive by the slightly less poor."

As the man farthest down, the least secure, the Negro was the hardest hit by this catastrophe. Economic misfortune was one product of the American system of which the Negro received his full share. Myrdal observed that all during the thirties public relief had become one of the major Negro occupations, being surpassed only by agriculture and possibly by domestic service.

Every investigation of the magnitude of human distress revealed that the Negro population was much worse off than everyone else. Such advances as they had been able to make during the previous decades had enchanced their self-respect and self-reliance but left them exposed to the misfortunes which can come through the coldly impersonal cruelties of the economic system.

When the Bureau of the Census finally got around to counting the unemployed in 1937 (after the peak had passed) they found that over a fourth of the Negro males and a third of the Negro females were looking for jobs but were unable to find them. Unemployment was more heavily concentrated in the North than in the South and was especially the characteristic of large cities. In some of these areas two-fifths of the Negro workers were idle.

Prejudice and discrimination are not entirely to blame for heavier unemployment rates among Negroes. They had not had time to establish themselves in industry and were without the protection of seniority. There was danger that the depression might cancel out the small gains they had been able to make in the preceding ten years.

The Negro was also more vulnerable to other causes of poverty. Chronically low incomes not only made it harder to live through periods of unemployment but also made it next to impossible to save for the years beyond the span of gainful work or other periods without income. The aged Negro in the South was, to some extent, cared for by his relatives and white friends. It was not uncommon for tenants who had spent a long time on a plantation to be allowed to stay on beyond their active span with the free use of a house and a patch of ground for vegetables and chickens and in other cases their children shared their little with them. But since he was engaged more in the heavy, hazardous jobs, crippling disability struck the Negro worker more often than the white man and the lack of funds for necessary medical care meant that a higher proportion of disability was not properly treated and became chronic, shortening the years of working life.

The Negro family was also more unstable. Desertion, divorce, and illegitimacy rates had always been high but did not cause much actual distress so long as women could obtain jobs as domestics so easily. Although the women heads of families could earn a living of a sort, life without a parent in the home all day was injurious for children. On many occasions on my house-to-house canvass in Athens, my knock at the door would be answered by a childish voice, "Mamma ain't here and we're locked in". But when the incomes of white families shrank, domestics could not be afforded and for this reason the incidence of unemployment among women workers was much higher than among men.

Since a greater proportion of Negroes were in need, their group benefited most by the emergency programs. A survey of relief in sample cities in 1934 showed that over half the Negro families in Northern cities were receiving relief and over a third of the families in Southern cities. This was in contrast with slightly over 10 percent of the white families in each region. When work relief replaced general relief, Works Progress Administration studies showed that, as late as 1941, even after the pick up of the defense effort, over two hundred thousand, or 16 percent of the workers assigned to Work Progress Administration, were Negroes—more than their proportion in the total population or in the unemployed population. The over-representation of the Negro in work relief was more pronounced in the North than in the South, but some of this discrepancy arose from the fact that in the rural South the Negro was cared for in part by the special farm programs.

It has also been claimed, with some justice, that the average relief grant and average work relief wage of Negroes in the South were lower than those for white recipients. This is often pointed to as another evidence of the reluctance of the South to even allow the Negro his share of the relief from misery. Such a sweeping conclusion is not entirely warranted. Relief grants and work wages are not intended to replace normal income fully, otherwise the temptation to make relief a profession would be too great for some people. Relief was granted on the basis of the minimum needs of the family, and work relief wages were geared to the prevailing wage of the community for the class of work assigned. So many Negro families were ineligible for relief because the breadwinner had a job and yet still lived so near the ragged edge of poverty that a high benefit for relief families would have given them incomes above many non-relief neighbors.

In 1935 the relief pattern changed. The nation had fully decided, in the words of Harry Hopkins, that "there is no need for any American to be destitute, to be illiterate, to be reduced by the bondage of these things into either political or economic impotence."

Accordingly, general relief was turned over to the States and the Works Progress Administration set up to carry on work relief until the economy had fully recovered. The social security system was inaugurated to build in guarantees that human misery would not again become so widespread. This system provides insurance against the hazards of temporary unemployment, old age, disability, premature death of workers, and assistance for the special categories of persons not normally eligible for insurance, the aged, the blind, dependent children, and permanently totally disabled.

A subtle but very real advantage which the Negro has gained from the operation of the Federal welfare programs as well as from minimum wage laws is that they are administered under acts and policies which, while flexible, do not permit discrimination on account of race. They are privileges which are based on the rights of the Negro as a citizen—not as a Negro citizen—but as an American whose misfortune has placed him along with other Americans who are ill-clothed, ill-housed and ill-fed.

In their early stages, the social insurances did not cover the whole working population. They excluded the self-employed, farmers, domestic servants, and teachers—occupations in which a large proportion of the Negro workers were engaged. Also benefits were determined on the basis of the previous wages of the worker. This meant that those in the lower wage brackets in general received lower benefits.

It should be repeated that these early disadvantages of the Negro under the social insurances arose, not because of his color, but because he was not in a favorable economic situation to be benefited. But the system has been constantly extended and perfected to the point that as it now operates a very large proportion of the Negro workers are eligible for protection under old age and survivors insurance, whose coverage has been extended to include domestics, farmers, the self-employed, and a substantial proportion of the teachers. On the other hand, the coverage of unemployment insurance has not been extended to these groups. In the event of another extended period of unemployment they will therefore be dependent on the special relief programs to keep the wolf from the door.

Partially because of lack of full insurance protection and partially because of greater need, the Negroes have always been over-represented with respect to their proportion in the total population among the recipients of special assistance. The proportion of Negroes receiving old age assistance, in 1953, was more than double the proportion of Negroes in the population 65 or more years of age. The incidence of need for aid to dependent children is especially high among Negroes. In 1953 the percent of Negro recipients of this type of aid was three times their percent in the population and in some states including a number in which Negroes are concentrated in cities, they constituted over half the case load.

Southern legislatures have never hesitated to appropriate as liberally as state finances would permit for aid to the aged, even though a large proportion of the grants have been for Negroes. Considerably more reluctance, however, is evidenced in their attitude toward aid to dependent children. A very substantial proportion of these funds is also for the benefit of Negroes and since it is well known that a high proportion of Negro applications are on behalf of children who are the victims of desertion or birth out of wedlock, there is strong opposition to this form of aid on the grounds that it might encourage immorality and subsidize illegitimacy—especially since an appreciable number of these mothers are repeaters. Some states have attempted to adopt legislation following the rule of baseball that "three strikes are out", but they have never been able to get around the Federal policy that the aid is granted for the child as well as the mother, and that the child should not be penalized for acts for which he was in no way responsible.

Stronger respect for the sanctity of the family is one need of the Negro which is a heritage of slavery and on which education and community action should be focussed. Some State Directors of Public Welfare tell me ruefully that they have tried to interest the Negro leaders in this problem with negligible results. They have the impression that the Negroes feel that it is in the hands of the government. But one did say that the colored women's clubs of a nearby city gave an annual testimonial dinner to girls who graduated from high school without a pregnancy. As I write these pages, the newspapers of Washington, D. C., are expressing shock and amazement at the reports of 95 girls under 16 years of age, mostly Negroes, who have within the last two years been excused from school on the grounds of pregnancy. This takes no account of the number over 16. The lack of organization in the Negro community for combating this laxness is also arousing local indignation.

It may well be that one adverse effect of the relief programs is to weaken the feeling of responsibility of Negro leaders for social problems and to create an unhealthy tendency for some colored and white people to abandon the traditional virtues of thrift and hard work and to lean too heavily on the government to absorb their troubles.

This attitude would be particularly understandable in the Negro because, ever since a major war was fought for his liberation, he has to some extent been treated as a ward of the nation and encouraged by some sympathizers to agitate and demand rather than to earn. There is scant evidence, however, that this dependence has greatly effected a larger segment of the Negro population than of the white except so far as it is used as a technique of Negro leaders to gain a disputed point. One can hardly blame a group, however, which has had so little in the past, for relying on every possible source of help and emphasizing rights rather than duties and responsibilities.

In addition to keeping the wolf from the door, the work programs kept the skills and work habits of the unemployed Negro from rotting away in idleness. They kept him as a standby labor reserve ready to meet the pressing need for manpower which was soon to be a prime necesity for winning a gruelling war.

The insurance and assistance programs are not substitutes for the traditional virtues of foresight and thrift. Neither do they constitute a full guarantee against freedom from want. They have, however, placed a substantial floor under American incomes and removed some of the haunting fear of the poor that misfortunes over which they have no control will cause their loved ones to go hungry or to shiver in unheated hovels.

CHAPTER 10

More and Better Jobs

The staggering production goals essential to win World War II called for the maximum efficient use of America's labor force, but old prejudices and roadblocks made it extremely difficult to realize the full potential of Negro workers. Some employers had become accustomed to a mixed labor force but these were chiefly the ones who needed labor for hot and heavy jobs. In most cases the Negroes were still excluded from the production line and confined to such minor places as porters, truck drivers and common laborers. There were still jobs which were labeled white and jobs labeled colored. There was no obstacle in the way of the white worker who chose to encroach on Negro territory but the opposition was formidable for a Negro who tried to move into a white occupation.

This pattern was a heritage from the Old South where the few skilled urban Negroes were mostly in the building trades. But the character of construction changed from small scale to large scale and with the change came new technologies. Unionization of the new processes barred Negroes from the new operations leaving them to work at the lower skilled, small scale jobs organized in separate unions. Otherwise they were occupied in ditch digging, street repair, railway maintenance, and as porters, janitors and domestics. The rapidly expanding Southern textile industry employed few Negro operatives.

The growing union movement, the attitudes of employers, and the sentiment of the community built a rigid compartment to restrict the Negro worker. This was true both in the South and in the North, the only difference being that in the South Negro wages were lower than white wages.

Even the initial modest gains of the Negro in industry were jeopardized by the depression. Industries which had bid for Negro labor when workers were scarce cut back their Negro force more rapidly than their white force when labor was plentiful. Skills began to rust and work habits to deteriorate.

The work programs of the Public Works Administration, the Works Progress Administration and of the Public Housing

Authority were particularly effective in creating temporary jobs for Negroes. About one-third of the low rent housing built was for Negro occupancy and the housing agency required that a minimum percentage of the skilled labor payroll should be allocated to Negroes, regardless of the occupancy of the dwellings.

Except in the early stages, when military cantonments were built, the skills of the building tradesmen were not the skills needed by America to win a highly technical modern war. Neither the white nor the Negro contingent of the labor force was ready to produce the mountains of specialized goods needed to support the kind of war that had to be fought. It appeared early that three-fourths of the new workers had to be skilled or semi-skilled. The economy was especially unprepared to make full utilization of Negro workers of this type, since this group not only had to be trained for new occupations, but had to be made acceptable to employers and fellow workers many of whom had a vested interest in keeping the color bar in industry intact.

Training programs of unprecedented size were set up all over the country. There were on-the-job training schools, vocational schools, and factory schools. The expanding aviation and ship-building industries required welders and riveters in greater numbers than could be quickly supplied. Small arms production, electrical equipment, and the more complex munitions required a host of new workers with a high degree of technical skill. Most of them had to be trained.

The Negro was particularly handicapped in fitting into this new industry first because of his previous lack of experience as a production worker and second because of the abysmal shortcomings of his pre-war vocational education opportunities. Since vocational education was the most expensive type it had been the most neglected by the Southern States. For a number of years the Federal Government had been making grants for vocational education in the public schools but the control of the types of education and the allocation of funds between the races were left to the states. As a result, vocational education in Negro schools received as inadequate a share of the money as general education. Such courses as were offered were mostly confined to home economics, agriculture, and the building trades. Money was not forthcoming to provide expensive mechanical equipment necessary to train workers for modern industry nor was there a supply of competent teachers to meet the need.

To the extent that the administration of war training programs was controlled by local public school authorities the usual pattern of neglect of Negroes continued into the first years of the defense effort. Plants which had not been in the habit of employing Negroes were reluctant to break with the tradition and admit them to in-plant training. Knowing the difficulties which confronted them in securing defense work, many Negroes were discouraged from registering for such courses as were offered.

The conclusion is inescapable that the Negro worker was the least prepared to adapt to the complex needs of the war effort and that his efforts to become prepared were beset with discouraging stumbling blocks.

The early years of the war were also marked by friction in the process of conversion. Plants were compelled to shift from non-essential to essential production and workers had to be shifted accordingly. The general policy was that such shifts should be made on the basis of seniority, but there was wide-spread resistance both on the part of management and of organized labor to the application of this policy to Negroes. Even in the industries which had become accustomed to the employment of large numbers of Negroes there was an effort to restrict them to common labor and janitorial jobs although this meant recruiting scarce white labor from the outside. Upgrading Negroes during conversion was especially resisted by those American Federation of Labor craft unions which had formerly excluded Negroes. The announced policy of the newly organized Congress of Industrial Organization was against racial discrimination but since it could not control its local affiliates strikes were often called when efforts were made to promote even a few Negroes to defense jobs on the basis of seniority. The situation was so troublesome that the manpower authorities were forced to threaten to fire the striking workers. Once the move was made, however, and Negroes proved to be satisfactory workers, the trouble evaporated.

Getting into newly established plants was also difficult for Negroes. Local employers were in the habit of requisitioning only white workers from the public employment service and in some instances these requests were filled without question.

In consequence there was a mass migration of white workers from non-defense areas to defense centers though the latter already had large pools of unemployed Negroes. This resulted in fantastic over-crowding and much wasteful movement. Houses were in exceedingly short supply, transportation systems burst at the seams and schools, restaurants, and recreation facilities were heavily overburdened. This community idiocy was typified by Charleston; although it had 4,000 unemployed Negroes it announced plans to bring in 9,000 more white workers.

The nation was engaged in a life and death struggle. Every ounce of productive effort was urgently needed and yet we almost reached the halfway point in the war before the firmly intrenched color barrier could be materially weakened. To foreign observers it must have been unbelievable that outworn traditional prejudices in industry could have persisted so stubbornly in the face of evermounting evidence of its futility and the pressing need to be rid of it.

The nation got itself into this tangle because of the relutance of management to break with tradition, the prejudice of some white employees against working by the side of Negroes, and the fear of job competition which was a carry-over from depression days.

In the early days of the war it was often difficult to determine who was most responsible for the under-employment of colored labor. In industries which operated without closed shop or union shop agreements it was obviously the responsibility of management to take the initiative in the hiring or promotion of Negro workers. But when pressure was applied by governmental agencies, management cited possible resistance of their regular employees and continued to insist that they should have priority to recruit white workers. And when organized labor had a voice in employment policies management claimed that union policies impeded the employment of Negroes.

It is, of course, impossible to generalize about the attitude of the unions. It varied from place to place and from industry to industry. Many forward looking leaders advocated full and immediate compliance with governmental policies; others were stubbornly adamant in their opposition.

To understand the opposition of organized labor to the Negro it is necessary to review some history. The first contacts of the Negro with trade unions came as a result of the drive to eliminate him or reduce his importance in certain skilled trades in which he had formerly had a virtual monopoly. We have seen how changes in the technology of building made it possible for white unions to gain control of the newer building crafts and to relegate

Negro carpenters and masons to lower paid jobs and in subordinate Negro locals. For fifty years the white railway brotherhoods had attempted by strategem or violence to displace Negroes from their traditional jobs as locomotive firemen. Finally, in this case also technology aided the accomplishment of their purpose. When mechanical stokers replaced hand firing of locomotives and later when diesels replaced steam, organized labor was able to secure agreements that gave white unions control of these operations and excluded the Negroes. Again when welding replaced riveting in ship construction, Negroes were pushed out of their skilled occupations in this industry. Thus whenever technological advance was made in a process on which Negroes worked, they were in danger of displacement.

When the first heavy waves of Negroes reached Northern cities they found themselves barred from many jobs in closed shops which were controlled by white unions. Under these circumstances it is understandable that when the white unions went on strike the Negroes welcomed the opportunity to gain a foothold as strikebreakers, but this hardly endeared them to organized labor. Also the long standing Southern policy of lower wages for Negroes gave them the reputation of cheap labor and there was a genuine fear on the part of white workers that the hiring of Negroes would pave the way for a reduction in wage scales.

By 1940 the previous liberal policy of the American Federation of Labor toward Negro labor had been reversed in favor of permission for internationals to organize separate Negro locals or affiliates. Some internationals, particularly in the metal trades, practiced outright exclusion. The Negro relegated to such subordinate status seldom had adequate grievance machinery, effective means of contract negotiation or job protection. The Congress of Industrial Organizations had been more unbiased in its initial approach to Negro labor but, because in its early stages, it was unable to control its locals there was strong opposition to the promotion of Negroes in defense work and in 1943 an epidemic of hate strikes resulted. So the Negro and organized labor faced their joint responsibility for winning the war with a strong mutual distrust—too strong to be swept aside by policy pronouncements alone or even by appeals to patriotism.

The combined pressures of all governmental agencies which were formulating policies for the recruiting and training of manpower were required to cajole or coerce war industries to make

full use of the neglected colored tenth of the labor force. Even so
Negro unemployment persisted into 1943, long after the bottom
of the white barrel had been scraped.

The pressures of the Office of Defense Management, War Production Board, and the War Manpower Commission were not
enough. These agencies all issued strong policy statements urging
non-discrimination but they had no teeth. The prejudiced elements of management and organized labor continued their policy
of hiring white men only or of token compliance by taking on a
few Negroes and assigning them to menial jobs. The war agencies
were also hampered initially by their unfamiliarity with the
problems involved and administrative ineptness in dealing with
a ticklish situation. The Negro was hampered by his pessimism
about being able to get a production job and was tempted to take
the first job that came along.

Progress was so alarmingly slow that President Roosevelt had
to act. In a memorandum to the Office of Production Management in June 1941 declared: "Our Government cannot counten-
ance continued discrimination against American citizens in defense production. Industry must take the initiative in opening the
doors of employment to all loyal and qualified workers regardless
of race, creed, color, or national origin. American workers, both
organized and unorganized, must be prepared to welcome the
general and much needed employment of fellow workers of all
races and nationality groups in defense industries."

This was immediately followed by the issuance of Executive
Order 8802 which reaffirmed the policy of full participation by
minorities in the defense program and gave it some teeth by
directing that all subsequent defense contracts should include
nondiscrimination clauses. The Committee on Fair Employment
Practice was set up under the order as a watchdog on discrimination and the backbones of other agencies which were dealing with
the labor supply were stiffened. Even so, another year was to
elapse before the administrative procedures could be perfected
during which time the Fair Employment Practice Committee was
compelled to cite some powerful corporations and influential
labor organizations before the recalcitrants began to realize that
the nation meant business and the spectre of cancellation of
juicy defense contracts brought about reasonably complete compliance.

Continued agitation on the part of Negro leaders, especially through the Urban League and the National Association for the Advancement of Colored People, and continually mounting demand for production finally opened the doors of war industry to Negro workers. In 1942, the situation eased slightly and during the following year considerable progress was made and finally by 1945 the Negro constituted eight percent of the employees in war plants.

The Negro economist, Robert C. Weaver, an outstanding authority on the subject, writes that during the war years more than a million Negroes entered civilian jobs. The number employed in skilled and semi-skilled occupations doubled. The proportion which Negro males constituted of all skilled workers increased to 3.6 percent and the percentage of semi-skilled operatives to over 10 percent. In the latter category the advance of Negro women was almost as rapid rising to over 8 percent of the total. The proportion of all employed Negro women who were in domestic service dropped from 60 to 45 percent. Many who left service in families found better paying opportunities in hotels, restaurants, and institutions.

This was a kitchen revolt which caused consternation among the former employers who had become accustomed to cheap servants. Something more tangible than the law of supply and demand had to be found to blame for the lack of household help, some sinister outside influence. An ideal scapegoat was at hand—Eleanor Roosevelt. During her husband's occupancy of the White House the First Lady had developed a genuine concern for colored people along with other disadvantaged groups, and she did not hesitate to let it be known. Accordingly, she became the symbol of the new dilemma of domestic service. The shortage in domestics was real but it gave rise to some wierdly fantastic tales, most entertaining to repeat over the teacups. "Eleanor" was reputed to have sponsored the organization of clubs variously known as "Daughters of Eleanor", "Eleanor Angel Clubs", "Sisters of Eleanor", and the "Royal House of Eleanor."

How the ex-Negro domestics must have chortled at the spectacle of their former employers relaying, in all seriousness, rumors like these: "Their motto is 'a white woman in every kitchen by Christmas." or "When a white woman asked a Negro woman to do her laundry she replied, 'All right, you come wash for me this week and I'll do yours next." This twaddle rolled so palatably on gossiping tongues that its variations were apparently unending and its spread unlimited. Given the reality of the new independence of Negro women and the deep distrust of the Roosevelt concern for the forgotten man, the popularity of this idiotic folklore is, in a way, understandable. It is one more bit of evidence of the willingness of the white people to clothe the reality of race relations with the glamour of half-truth.

The heaviest employment of colored workers continued to be in iron and steel production, but substantial numbers had entered the production of aluminum, tanks, shipbuilding, ammunition, ordnance, and tires with a scattering representation in a wide range of other defense establishments. "These changes in a period of four years," as Weaver comments, "represented more industrial and occupational diversification for Negroes than had occurred in the seventy-five preceding years. . . . They also permitted some Negroes to work alongside white workers in many individual establishments on the basis of industrial equality."

Management had discovered the soundness of the principle that maximum labor productivity could be attained only by the assignment of workers on the basis of experience and skill and not by an inflexible restriction of any group to Jim Crow departments or jobs. Scores had found by experience the truth stated by the personnel manager of a large war plant when he said: "Industry is finding that it is more profitable to upgrade Negro janitors to semi-skilled or skilled jobs than to train white workers from outside the plant. Likewise, it is more profitable to use the unemployed Negroes in the community than to import white workers from other cities. Gradually we are becoming aware that the production demands of this war can be met only by skills and by manpower recruited, trained, up-graded, and fully utilized regardless of race, creed, color, nationality, sex or age."

A large segment of management had learned that all that is necessary to make such an arrangement effective is to announce a firm policy, plan its inauguration thoroughly, educate the supervisory personnel, and appeal to the fairness of the rank and file of workers.

Organized labor was learning that white and Negro workers could and did work side by side without friction and that in a period of full employment the hiring of Negroes did not take any jobs away from white men. The Negro was realizing that organized labor need not necessarily be his enemy but could on occasion be a very powerful ally; and he was learning the technique of participation in the modern labor movement. Heartening from the viewpoint of labor, the Negro, and the public are the findings of John Hope in his recent study *Equality of Opportunity*, dealing with the practices and policies of the United Packinghouse Workers relating to racial discrimination.

Such lessons have not been completely or universally learned. There are still employers, especially in the South, who are distinctly reluctant to hire Negroes except in menial jobs. There are numerous union locals, North and South, unwilling to accept Negro members. The recent resurgence of bitterness following the desegregation decision of the Supreme Court caused many threats of discharge for Negroes active in antisegregation movements; a few white locals, partially under the influence of the hate organizations, have threatened to form new labor unions rather than allow Negroes to join the existing groups.

The merger of the A. F. of L. and the C. I. O. into one organization was followed by the announcement of an intensified recruiting drive, particularly in the South, but this has been slowed up by race prejudice. It will require more years of experience and more education of workers and employers before the full productivity of the Negro labor force is developed.

I know of only a few American economists who did not confidently expect a business recession when industry was reconverted from war to peace production in 1945. One of the popular Washington pastimes in which I participated in the later years of the war was known as post-war planning. By direction of the President we hastily assembled a shelf of public works for emergency employment purposes. We sweated over a Service Man's Readjustment Act designed to cushion the shock for demobilized soldiers and to keep as many of them as possible occupied in school until the economy recovered enough to absorb them.

But the emergency never came. Business men had been doing some post-war planning of their own without benefit of governmental auspices. They had their eyes on the pent-up demand arising from war scarcities and the savings accumulated from war wages. Moreover, county and city governments were eager to go ahead with construction which war shortages had held back. In addition, demobilized military personnel, both colored and white, proceeded to take advantage of the GI educational benefits in gratifying numbers and were able to obtain the kind of training for industry which civilians had received during the war. Better still, jobs were waiting for the GI's when they finished school. Reconversion went smoothly and a period of prosperity and full employment began.

The extent to which Negro workers have been able to hold on to their wartime gains in city occupations is indexed by their status in 1950. At that time only about a fourth of the Negro males were employed in agriculture. The others, numbering almost 2.5 million, included nearly 250,000 professional, clerical and sales personnel, more than 250,000 skilled craftsmen, almost 750,000 semi-skilled operatives, and 1,250,000 service workers and common laborers.

Their rise in status has been accompanied by a rise in income. The National Recovery Administration struck the first blow at discriminatory wages in the South. This was followed by the federal minimum wage law, a measure enforced without regard to color. Although many Negro jobs have not been subject to the minimum wage law, the competition for workers in the higher-wage occupations has forced increases in wages in jobs not covered. Thus, Negro farm labor and domestics now receive much higher pay than before World War II. The years from 1940 to 1955 have been called the golden age of the American Negro for never before has he come so near getting his share of the prosperity of a fabulously prosperous nation.

One of the symbols of progress is the ownership of a large, shiny automobile—the larger and shinier the better. I now live on the edge of a fairly prosperous Negro neighborhood and the number of second hand Cadillacs and Buicks is astounding. A friend tells me of a visit to the town of Louisville, Georgia, where the old slave auction block has been preserved in the court house square. While he was examining this relic of the past a Negro woman drove up in a large car, conspicuously circled the square several times and drove off.

But more substantial progress is indicated by the increase in homeownership to the point that one of every three Negro city families live in owned homes.

Although a disproportionately large number of Negroes are still in the lower-income groups an increasingly large number are appearing in the middle-income range and tending to acquire the habits, the tastes, the dress and the homes of middle-class America.

CHAPTER 11

Comrades in Arms

The career of Toussaint L'Ouvertoure who, with hunger and disease as allies, pushed some of Napoleon's crack troops unceremoniously out of Haiti and established a Negro republic on that island has long fascinated me. Some of his generals and officers had received their baptism of fire during the American Revolution, and probably sharpened their zeal for liberty in the siege of Savannah when they gallantly protected the retreat of Compte D' Estaing after his repulse by the British. Alexander Dumas, the son of a mulatto who was one of Napoleon's more spectacular generals, remains one of my favorite authors.

While visiting New England several years ago I saw the monument on Boston Common which honors Crispus Attucks. The *Encyclopedia Americana* refers to him as a Negro, mulatto or an Indian, probably an escaped slave. The event for which he is commemorated is the leadership of his fellow townsmen in the Boston Massacre of 1770 an occasion which gave the British a preview of the Revolution which was soon to follow. Whatever else he might have been, Crispus Attucks was not white. But he was the first to fall in this rioting and thus gained the title of the first patriot to die in the American cause.

When the continental militias were mustered for the Revolution they contained quite a sprinkling of black faces. A Negro, Prince Whipple, was in Washington's boat crossing the Delaware.

In his diary Baron Von Closen says of his visit to an American Revolutionary war encampment at White Plains, "one-fourth of the troops were Negroes and all looked cheerful and well. It was the regiment from Rhode Island that I found the smartest and best disciplined. Three-fourths of this regiment were Negroes." One suspects that in those days, when it was possible to avoid military service by hiring a substitute, some colonists accomplished this by sending their slaves which were scattered throughout the thirteen colonies.

It was natural to make use of the acting talent of Negroes in the role of patriot spies. The capture of Stony Point was made easy for Anthony Wayne by Pompey Lamb, who, in the guise of a vegetable huckster, scouted the defenses thoroughly. After securing the password and permission to return at night, he smuggled in two soldiers, also disguised as hucksters; they overcame the guards and paved the way for a bloodless capture of a seemingly impregable position. Others who used their wits to wander in and out of the British lines were James Amistead, who warned LaFayette of a planned surprise attack; James Honeyman, who received his freedom by act of the Rhode Island legislature for similar service; and an unnamed garrulous Negro who deceived the British into thinking they faced a disorganized, weak American force at Edenton when, in fact, it was well prepared to repulse their attack.

In the War of 1812 Andrew Jackson addressed his contingent of free Negroes with these words: "Soldiers, from the shores of Mobile I collected you to arms; I invited you to share the perils and to divide the glory with your white countrymen. I expected much from you, for I was not uniformed as to those qualities which must render you so formidable to an invading foe. I know that you loved the land of your nativity, and that, like ourselves, you had to defend all that is most dear to man; but you surpass my hopes. I have found in you, united to those qualities, that noble enthusiasm which impels to great deeds." After the battle of New Orleans he singled out his Negro troops for praise.

The early navies included a larger proportion of Negroes than the armies. Pilots were especially valued for their knowledge of coastal waters. The Surgeon on Commodore Perry's ship in 1816 reported that one in six or eight of the seamen were Negroes.

Negroes were not recruited extensively in the Civil War until after the Emancipation Proclamation in 1863. Scattering use of Negro volunteers had been made before that but the federal government was reluctant to sacrifice any lingering hope of reconciliation with the South and rejected most early offers of Negro volunteers. On the Confederate side there are also scattered references to free Negro volunteers but in the main the Southerners were averse to training slaves to use firearms until the very end of the war. Not until they were scraping the bottom of the barrel for men, did they propose the recruiting of Negroes. Nevertheless, at the outset, the Third Alabama left for the front with 1,000 white troops and 400 Negro body servants.

National recruiting began in Massachusetts where two Negro regiments were organized. There also stands on Boston Common a monument to Colonel Robert Gould Shaw who commanded one of these units, the 54th Massachusetts volunteers. They served with distinction in the attack on Fort Wagoner, outside of Charleston, and Colonel Shaw was killed in this engagement.

At the battle of Milliken's Bend, General Grant reported: "In this battle, most of the troops engaged were Africans, who had but little experience in the use of firearms. Their conduct is said, however, to have been most gallant."

Soon after volunteers were called for by the Union, 185,000 had enlisted. An equal number were included within the lines as labor troops and miscellaneous units. Although late in enlisting, many Negro units were trained in time to serve creditably in a number of engagements.

In spite of this outstanding record of Negro troops in the Revolution, the War of 1812, and the Civil War, there was still much hesitancy about enlisting them in the regular army. After the Civil War Congress provided that four Negro regiments be activated. These were the 9th and 10th Cavalries and the 24th and 25th Infantries which served with dash and favor in the Indian Wars, the Spanish-American War, and the Mexican expedition. The Indians called them Buffalo Soldiers and considered them "bad medicine", in their twenty-five year patrol of the plains they established a reputation for good discipline, hard fighting and superb horsemanship.

When Teddy Roosevelt made his celebrated charge up San Juan hill his Rough Riders were included along with the units of the Negro regiments in the command of Fighting Joe Wheeler. Wheeler was a famous ex-Confederate cavalryman who was known to sometimes forget which war he was in. Once he led his men with a rebel yell shouting: "Come on, boys, we've got the dammed Yankees on the run!" In writing of the 10th Cavalry afterwards Wheeler pointed out that "the reports of all their commanders unite in commending the Negro soldier."

After modern warfare outmoded the use of cavalry, the 9th and 10th were disbanded but the 24th and 25th infantries continued on through World War II. The 24th topped off its career as an all Negro outfit by winning our first major Korean victory at Yechon.

Immediately after American entry in World War I, the French were most insistent that some American units be assigned to them as a token that Americans were ready. The American Expeditionary Force was training to act as a unit, but four Negro regiments were assigned to the French fairly soon. One of these was from the New York National Guard, one from the Illinois Guard and the other two from miscellaneous sources. No artillery was available to send with these troops so they were "brigaded" with French regiments and French artillery. Thus when Pershing landed and said, "Lafayette we are here." Those Negroes were also there right away. They were designated the 93rd Division.

The French wanted these troops badly because they were desperately in need of every man that could be found to check the relentless German advances. They were therefore sent to the front lines almost immediately and one regiment served in the trenches for 192 days without relief, not losing a foot of ground or a single prisoner. Another participated with the French in saying "they shall not pass" at Verdun.

For every Negro infantryman, however, there were dozens of supply troops and auxiliaries. War was becoming more complex and mountains of supplies had to be shipped and stored. A butcher batallion was recruited from the stock yards and bakery companies from various sources. The unloading of American ships which streamed into Brest and St. Nazaire was congenial work for Negro stevedores and many a Southern white boy, myself included, was made homesick on arrival in France by the rythmic, rolling work songs of these singing soldiers.

Later another complete Negro combat division, the 92nd, was sent to France in time to see some action in the Argonne and participate in some of the bloody preliminary attacks on Metz which terminated by the signing of the armistice before they had time to demonstrate fully their ability.

But the fortunes of war do not always follow the American eagle, especially when the enemy is as tough a customer as the German. Rumors began to float around the A. E. F. that the 92nd had "chickened" in battle and was to be sent home. It was typical of the Army that the 93rd, which was doing splendidly was never mentioned, but that the 92nd, which had one reverse, was a target for rumor mongers. Being on duty at General Headquarters, I was in a position to sift fact from fancy. Much of the common gossip was based on sheer fancy. However, rumors persisted long after the armistice even though they were denounced by the Commanding General and the Secretary of War.

In brief the 92nd was shipped over to France poorly trained both as to officers and privates. While still green it was, through poor overhead staff work, placed in an impossible position and did lose some ground initially but came back later to redeem itself. In writing of this action, General C. C. Ballou said:

"An infantry regiment, never before in battle, was detached from the division . . . placed between the French and American armies, in a gap so wide that they were out of touch with both and there during the night, under the influence of a bombardment to which they could not reply because of the limitation of their weapons, the battalion in the front lines very generally, but not entirely, drifted to the rear, but not in a stampede." Of this incident, the French general said: "It was a difficult situation—one that would have tested the quality of experienced troops of tested valor." This was enough to condemn the memory of the 92nd eclipsing their later performance before Metz when, after more training and experience, they advanced stubbornly in heavily fortified territory.

The 92nd must be somewhat a Jonah for they were involved in a similar incident in the Italian campaign which is also the subject of some controversy between high-ranking generals. In this case, however, the adverse criticism was not enough to offset the fine record which Negro troops, as a whole, were making in all theatres of World War II.

All this adds up to the fact that fighting ability is not a question of race but of training, motivation and leadership. These things lead me to believe that there is much truth in the military maxim that there are no poor soldiers, but many poor officers.

The willingness of these colored boys to go along in war was all the more remarkable since many of them did not have too clear an idea of what they might be facing and what the shooting was all about. I remember vividly that the transport on which I went to France also carried a Negro battalion—very seasick and homesick most of the time. Their station for abandoning ship was next to mine. After lining up several times for practice drills the time came when there was some threat of danger. The lookout had sighted a submarine or empty barrel or something else that looked like a submarine and just as we lined up at our abandon ship stations the stern gun took a crack at it. As soon as he heard this, one of the Negroes, probably thinking of nothing else than that he might never eat agin, threw his mess kit far over the side of the ship saying "I know I am not going to need this any more and I am going to swim light."

Then there was Horace whom we were trying to steer through the draft board. The clerk of the board, knowing that Horace couldn't read or write, was being very helpful by explaining the questions to him. When she came to the question: "Are you a conscientious objector?" Horace said "Yes mam, I am a good conscientious objector." Somewhat taken back, she asked, "Now Horace do you know what a conscientious objector is?" He replied "I am not so sure, but I know he is a good fellow." She said "No Horace, a conscientious objector is a man who doesn't believe in fighting", and Horace commented: "No ma'm that is not me, I love to fight."

The last thing which would be admitted by the ardent advocate of white supremacy is that some elements in the South have a lurking fear of the Negro. Their inability to recognize this fear arises from the fact that it is for the most part subconscious. It shows clearly, however, whenever crises occur and its most persistent manifestation is in the uncritical belief of baseless rumors and the speed with which these tall tales spread.

War brings on the type of crisis psychology which is particularly hospitable to rumor. There is something about the Negro in uniform which gives the more ignorant Southerner a first class case of jitters and spawns the most absurd fantasies.

There are stories of what the Negro in uniform will do, stories of what he won't do. There are stories of what the Negro who stays home will do and won't do.

I have described, in the paragraphs above, some of the rumors which I encountered during World War I as they were circulated in the Army. Since I was in France at the time I did not have the benefit of the rumors that kept the home fires burning. They must have been pretty bad; otherwise the Ku Klux would not have found such a fertile field for its activities. However, I encountered most of the World War II varieties of rumor. Some are worth a wholesome belly laugh.

Many stories revolved around the policy of draft boards. Either that too many Negroes were being drafted and would return home with inflated ideas and combat training and try to take over; or too few were being taken and that when the maximum number of white men were overseas the Negroes left would rise and take control.

There was another crop whose base was plainly sex fear. The University of North Carolina Press publication, *Race and Rumors of Race*, contains the following samples of this type.

From South Carolina came a rumor that "when white men go to the Army, the Negro men will have the white women." In North Carolina it was said that "Negro men are all planning to have white wives." In Georgia it was reported that a fight between whites and Negroes was supposedly caused by a Negro who was overheard saying to a friend, "Aren't we going to have a time with all these white women, when all these white men go off to war."

In accepting these rumors little thought was given to the actual fact that only a small proportion of white men were being taken into the army or even to the possibility that the white women might have some say in the matter.

Still another explosive type of rumor catalogued by the North Carolina study pertained to predictions of violent interracial outbreaks. One which spread from one end of the South to the other was the "ice pick" story: "They say that Negroes are buying up ice picks to attack the whites". There was also a rumor that Negroes were planning to take over the entire area during a blackout in September. Such stories were often embellished with great circumstantial detail: "A Negro undertaking establishment began to buy a great many coffins. The shipments were so large and so numerous that the suspicions of the stationmaster were aroused and he reported the matter to the sheriff. The sheriff went to the station to see the next shipment, but he made it seem as if he were visiting the stationmaster. He accidently turned one of the coffins over and found it to be full of guns. Upon investigation, the undertaking establishment was found to be a cache of guns which were to have been used in a Negro rebellion."

The Negroes, who more than any one else were in a position to see how baseless these rumors were, would probably have seen the humorous side of the spectacle of the superior white man in such a jittery state if they had not been so keenly aware of the danger of violent reprisal that such inflammatory stories kept alive. Then, too, they were busy spreading some pretty wild stories of their own. In going into battle, it was widely rumored each white soldier was to have a Negro soldier in front of him.

Although such stories were patently ridiculous, their existence was distinctly tragic. False as they were these stories were a social fact, intensifying tension to the danger point at a crucial period in history when a great segment of the nation was embarking upon a task which required sacrifice, heroism, and above all unity.

It is fortunate indeed that when the draft call was issued for World War II there was a general realization that if Negroes were drafted along with whites they would not enter wholeheartedly into the defense of the American way of life if they had to wear the badge of segregation in the armed forces.

Officers training schools were integrated from the beginning, thereby eliminating the chance of inferior training and motivation of Negro officers. The Marine Corps ended its long tradition of "for white only." By the end of the war it had absorbed 20,000 Negroes with such good results that after Saipan the Commandant of the Corps announced: "The Negro Marines are no longer on trial. They are Marines."

Only first steps to integration were made during the war. It was not until after the armistice that a series of administration pressures led to a critical reappraisal of the tradition of separate units which had been the basis of military policy for nearly 100 years. As a result, separate Negro units were abolished, training programs integrated, and the principle of assignment by merit established. This much progress has been made without any of the bad reactions which had been predicted. However, the rate of advance of the various services has been uneven. There are still complaints about difficulties due to civilian personnel practices.

In a report on integration in the armed services in 1955 the Assistant Secretary of Defense stated:

"The Negro citizen in the armed forces is now being utilized on the basis of individual merit and proficiency in meeting the needs of the services.

"Throughout the Army, Navy, Air Force, and Marine Corps fully integrated units have replaced the all-Negro units which, until recent years, formed the only channel of military service for Negro enlistees and draftees since Colonial times.

"Thorough evaluation of the battle-tested results to date indicates a marked increase in overall combat effectiveness through integration.

"Economies in manpower, materiel, and money have resulted from the elimination of racially duplicated facilities and operations.

"The program has advanced more rapidly than had been considered possible in some quarters, and there have been no untoward incidents."

There is therefore reason to hope that by the time the next war comes—if it must come—the enemy will find America more united than ever and not with a tenth of its soldiers distrustful of the ideals which they are called on to defend.

CHAPTER 12

Helping Hands for the South

Thomas Jefferson's bill for the more general diffusion of knowledge was the beginning of a long struggle to establish public schools in the South. Although he succeeded in getting the University of Virginia chartered, he spent the last twenty-five years of his life trying in vain to persuade his state to establish public schools for the lower grades. Toward the close of his life he remarked that if he had been given a choice between the university and "primaries", he would have chosen the "primaries".

The people were not ready for public schools in Jefferson's time. There had been some free schools in the colonies for paupers and orphans, attaching the stigma of charity to public education. Other schools were sponsored by the churches or religious institutions. Well-to-do families educated their children in the home. The larger antebellum mansions set aside school rooms where tutors or family members instructed the children, sometimes including the offspring of the Negro house servants. It had not become customary for mammas to get their children out from under foot by parking them in school for most of the day.

Strongly opposed to taxation, the landed gentry argued that they should not be penalized to educate the children of the man without property. Thus education in those days was much like medical care today. The rich could afford it, the poor could have it free of charge, and the middle class was left out.

As a substitute for taxation literary or library funds were established to pay for the tuition of poor children and to help support various types of schools. These funds were state-chartered institutions which received donations, bequests and the income of miscellaneous property which reverted to the state.

Partial public support was extended to academies which served as college preparatory institutions before the Civil War. Some of these academies became widely famous because they sent excellently prepared students to their own state universities as well as to the universities of the North. Their education was not of the "deluxe" variety. As one of the academies was described: "The houses were little log huts, with chimneys built of sticks chinked with mud. . . . The street was about forty yards wide and the houses, ten or twelve ranged on the sides, either built by the students themselves or by architects hired by them. . . . At the head of the street stood the academy, differing in nothing from the other buildings but size. There were two rooms in this, one for the primary pupils, while the larger was the recitation room of Dr. Waddel himself, the prayer room, court room and general convocation room for all matters pertaining to the school. It was without seats and just large enough to contain one hundred and fifty boys standing erect, close pressed."

But academy instruction was thorough. "Under the wide spreading branches in the summer, and in their huts in the winter, the students diligently studied, changing their occupations at the sound of a horn, and repairing to the house for recitation when called for by the name of 'the Virgil Class', 'the Homer class', etc. In a moment they appear before their preceptor, and with order and decorum recite their lessons—are carefully examined in grammar and syntax—the construction of sentences—the formation of verbs—the antiquities of Greece and Rome—the history and geography of the ancients."

Several hundred academies were scattered through the South. Together with the local "old field" and church schools, they constituted the educational system below college grade. However, some scattered beginnings of public schools were made shortly before the Civil War. Several states managed to secure a little income from the land grants set aside by the federal government and it was supplemented with scanty tax funds.

As a result of the Civil War Southern education almost came to a complete halt. Many of the academies were destroyed. The literary funds were bankrupted since most of their investments had been in Confederate bonds. Taxable property values practically disappeared, and corrupt officials looted the state treasuries. The whole social and economic fabric of the region was torn to tatters and rebuilding had to start literally from the ground up.

The conquered Southern states were required to rewrite their constitutions before they could be readmitted to the Union. All of the reconstruction constitutions contained provision for public schools, and a halfhearted start was made to establish them but, since this measure was imposed on the South by military government, it was bitterly resented. These constitutions provided for a high degree of centralization of control of the schools which was also distrusted. Although non-segregated schools were not required by law, the reconstruction governments tried to impose them in some states. This, too, was bitterly resented. As a result, when the military governments were withdrawn, the Southern States repealed their reconstruction constitutions. Although the public school provisions generally remained on the statute books, the distracted and impoverished people did not have the will or the means to get them going. The sparseness of the rural population also presented difficulties. In consequence Southern education remained at an exceedingly low ebb until about 1885.

The struggle to get a start in Negro education was still more difficult but it was assisted by helping hands from the rest of the nation. As the Civil War progressed, more and more liberated slaves and refugees piled up behind the Union lines. Schools were started by the military authorities and the Freedmen's Bureau. The earliest, Penn Normal and Industrial School, was opened in 1862 by two dedicated missionaries after the Union forces occupied St. Helena Island midway between Charleston and Savannah. On this island thousands of slaves had been deserted when their masters fled before the Union troops,

About 70 years after its founding I had the opportunity to spend a year on St. Helena Island and observe the way in which the Penn Normal School had built a Negro community. There had still been so little contact between the island and the mainland that the local "Gullah" dialect was almost unintelligible to the outsider. At the time of my visit the island had some 6,000 Negroes and 200 whites. Most of the Negroes were landowners who showed much pride in their small, neat homes. They had developed a self-sustaining agriculture in spite of depressions and natural calamities. The interests of the farmers and homemakers were promoted by the farm and home demonstration agents. The sheriff rarely bothered to visit the island since it had no major crimes and petty disputes were "tried" in churches. It was a fairly healthy community with no tuberculosis, a fairly low infant mortality, and few epidemics—thanks to the efforts of a school nurse and a Negro doctor. It was a self-respecting, self-sustained community, the product of two generations of free Negroes under the leadership of the school. How different would the South of today be had there only been several hundred such community schools after the Civil War.

The most widely-known of the schools founded by the Freedmen's Bureau were Howard University in Washington, D. C., which has continued under the auspices of the federal government as a national Negro university, and Hampton Institute, a trade, agriculture, and teacher training school in Virginia.

A number of other important schools were established by Northern missionary organizations. Many of them are substantial institutions today. The American Missionary Association of the Congregational Church founded Atlanta University, Fisk University and several small schools. The American Baptist Home Mission Society established Morehouse College, Shaw University and quite a few others. Unfortunately, these missionary efforts were, in the Southern mind, associated with the carpetbag government and, as a result, the schools they created were not accepted as a part of Southern life. However, they were tremendously valuable in beginning to train sorely needed Negro teachers for the public schools which were to come later. Moreover, the white missionary teachers in these institutions became a vital link between white people and the growing numbers of educated Negroes.

Southern Negroes also joined in the effort to promote their own education. Their church groups organized numerous small schools throughout the South; some of them have grown into substantial colleges, aided in some degree by donations from Southerners. The only missionary effort of the White South for the Negro was represented by Paine College in Augusta, Georgia—a joint enterprise of the Southern Methodist and Colored Methodist Espiscopal Zion churches.

Since all of these schools were privately supported, they subsisted on a precarious income. Negroes were too poor to pay much tuition, most of the boarding departments operated at a loss, and the range of subjects taught was severly limited by the small faculties and inadequate laboratory equipment. The finances of Negro demoninational schools were especially precarious since they had to depend on collections of nickles, dimes and quarters solicited from poor folk. Elementary education for the masses was too much of a job for these private institutions and as public schools strengthened the private effort concentrated more on high school and college training, developing special facilities in agricultural, industrial, and teacher training.

Public education in the South also received stimulation from private philanthropy. This was especially true of Negro education. Aid to education came through cooperation of both Northern and Southern leaders. In spite of the traditional prejudice against, and apathy toward public education, a small number of great-hearted Southerners began early to devote themselves to its development.

Big business in that day was also eager to hire military heroes. Robert E. Lee was offered a handsome salary by a national business concern which had substantial connections in the South. However, he refused the offer and instead accepted the Presidency of Washington College, an institution which later became Washington and Lee University. In his reply to the offer he stated that he had led the sons of the Confederacy into battle and wanted to spend the rest of his life leading them in the paths of education. In every state in the South strong men appeared to take up the same cause. There was a feeling that giants were walking abroad and exhorting the region to lift itself by its own bootstraps.

Efforts of these early pioneers were reinforced by the Peabody Education Fund. George Peabody, a man from Massachusetts who had made some of his money in business in the South, and added to it as an international banker set aside three million dollars for education in the South. Of this one million dollars was in Confederate bonds which were later repudiated, but two million dollars remained. In those days when dollars were uninflated this amount gave an appreciable lift to education at a time when it was most needed.

Another helping hand from the North was extended by Robert C. Ogden who saw the need of getting the Southern educators together to encourage and reinforce one another. Since they worked in separate states, they did not have much opportunity for contact with others. Ogden organized the Conference for Education in the South, inviting outstanding leaders to annual meetings to which he brought many influential Northern people as guests in his private car. Many genuine, influential, and wealthy friends of education in the South were assembled in this way.

In the meantime General Armstrong, who had founded Hampton Institute, had been succeeded by Hollis B. Frissell who was truly a genius at handling people. Frissell's ambition for Hampton was not only to train tradesmen and teachers, but above all to instil character in freedmen which would enable them to meet the competition of a free world. He was a strict disciplinarian, deeply religious, and meticulously thorough. He was known to the students as "Old Struggle" because of his insistence that the good things of life only came through struggle. One of his favorite quotations was "From the idle rich and the lazy poor may the good Lord deliver us." Frissell's method was to work behind the scenes and promote progress by knowing who should be persuaded to spearhead a movement.

With Frissell and the Southern educators as idea men and Northern philanthropists to provide funds a genuine ferment for public education was set to work.

Another remarkable character among the financiers recruited by Ogden was George Foster Peabody (no kin to the George Peabody who was mentioned above). Born in Georgia, this Peabody was reared by a family with scant means. After the Civil War he made his way to New York and soon became immensely wealthy as an investment banker and as a titan in big business. Among other things he loaned Edison his first $10,000.

When the Conference for Education in the South, organized mainly for promotion and propaganda, formed the Southern Education Board which was designed to make grants and engage in active programs, Mr. Peabody became its treasurer. Soon strong Negro leaders were added to this combination. Booker T. Washington had been trained at Hampton and gone down to Alabama to establish Tuskegee Institute and other Negro educators also were becoming known and influential.

At first there was some complaint from some of the white educators that too much attention was being given to Negro education. The Southern Education Board, however, held steadfastly to its policy that education in the South was for all Southerners, whatever their color, and the laggards soon began to fall in line.

Thus public schools in the South which were started some twenty years after the surrender at Appamatox began to get some popular support and financial backing from state legislatures. Much of the early success is traceable to the wholehearted cooperation of these educational pioneers.

The South continued to receive assistance for Negro education all during the first half of this century. The most substantial amounts came from the General Education Board, founded by John D. Rockefeller, whose grants to this corporation, together with investment income from 1902 to 1947, totalled over a quarter of a billion dollars; of this, over a hundred and twenty-five million was allocated to education in the South and over fifty million to the education of the Negro. The most substantial amounts went to universities, colleges, and secondary schools but considerable sums were also granted for public schools and numerous fellowships, scholarships, and grants which were of inestimable value in preparing leaders for Southern education.

Mr. Rockefeller was as hard headed in giving his money away as he had been in earning it. His philosohpy was that "money which comes to a man without effort on his part is seldom a benefit and often a curse . . . but if we can help people help themselves then there is a permanent blessing conferred." Early in its operation the General Education Board secured Wallace Buttrick as its Secretary and Executive Officer. He was a man of exceptional vision and diplomacy, truly an educational statesman.

His vision and tact in dealing with the South is embodied in his address to the joint session of the Georgia legislature soon after the board was organized: "We had not proceeded far in this study before we became convinced that our energies should be directed chiefly to the promotion of education in the rural districts. . . . We also saw that a great need was for the preparation of teachers for these rural schools, and we therefore resolved that a considerable part of our work should be that of cooperating with normal schools and with other schools prepared to train teachers. We decided that the only proper avenue of approach to the public schools of a state was through its state department of public instruction. We do not for a moment contemplate an independent campaign for education. We have no thought of colonizing northern teachers in the South, or of propagating northern ideas at the South; quite the contrary, we believe that the teachers of the South must be people of the South, and that your schools must be organized and maintained by you in harmony with your institutions and traditions."

In line with this policy one of the General Education Board's principal contributions to Negro education was to make available to the State Department of Education the funds to employ state supervisors of Negro schools. They were fortunate in enlisting some of the ablest and most sympathetic young educators of the region for this work. In addition to the usual contacts with county superintendents in developing the basic elements of Negro education, the supervisors provided a central point in each state for the promotion and administration of the programs of other foundations specifically interested in Negro education.

As early as 1882, the interest of John F. Slater, of Connecticut, was attracted by the success of the Peabody Fund and he donated a million dollars, the income "of which was to be used to assist in the education of the Negro people of the Southern States." The first director was Dr. Atticus Haygood, of Atlanta, a Southerner of fine stock. He had just been elected bishop of the Southern Methodist Episcopal Church but resigned in order to accept the directorship of the Slater Fund. After Bishop Haygood, the Slater Fund was administered by a succession of similarly dedicated men with a remarkable blend of idealism and practical common sense. The first problem which they determined to attack was of the preparation of sorely needed teachers. Initially private and higher institutions were aided for this purpose. Dr. James H. Dillard, who later combined under his direction the Jeanes and Slater Funds, reoriented the teacher training activities to reach closer to the grass roots. Highly successful experiments were made in establishing county training schools which added teacher training to the elementary and high school subjects in one of the county schools. These were to be parts of the public school system, supported largely from public funds. This work was so successful and met such a basic need that the income from the Slater Fund was, from time to time, supplemented by other foundations, notably the General Education Board, Rosenwald Fund, Peabody Fund and Carnegie Foundation. This varied support meant that the establishment of one of these county training schools became a cooperative enterprise. Some were aided by as many as seven sources—the state, the county, private subscriptions, the Slater Fund, the General Education Board, the Rosenwald Fund and the Smith-Hughes appropriations for vocational education.

Another happy combination of Northern money and Southern ideas was exemplified by the Anna T. Jeanes Fund. At the solicitation of George Foster Peabody and Hollis B. Frissell, Anna T. Jeanes, a devout Quaker, became intensely interested in aiding rural schools, another practical need. When she signed the endowment fund of a million dollars over to the trustees she said to Dr. Frissell in her quaint way: "Dost thee remember when thee came I gave thee $10,000 for Negro schools. And then I gave thee $200,000 more. Now I am giving all for the little schools. This is a great privilege. I am just a poor woman, and I give not to save my soul, but just because I wanted to."

When the donation came the idea was ready. Jackson Davis, the superintendent of schools of Henrico County, Virginia, had discovered in one of his rural schools, Virginia Randolph, a Negro teacher of unusual ability, who had made her school distinctly superior in every way to the surrounding schools especially in the common industrial and domestic arts. She obtained permission to visit some of the other teachers and assist them to raise the standard of their work with the result that many of the rural schools underwent an outstanding transformation. When Davis reported on this work to Dr. James H. Dillard, who was administering the Jeanes Fund, Dillard began to extend the supervising teacher plan gradually to other counties. There were soon so many calls on the Jeanes Fund for assistance of this type that its insufficient income had to be supplemented by the Phelps-Stokes Fund and others.

Incidentally, Jackson Davis, who ably assisted Virginia Randolph in spreading her idea, later became the first State supervisor of Negro schools under the program of the General Education Board, and still later general field agent and director of that Board.

The Jeanes and Slater Funds have now been merged with the Virginia Randolph Fund and the residual of the Peabody Fund. They operate within the Southern Education Foundation which continues the excellent work of the constituent funds in strengthening the work of the rural teachers and principals, in making grants and aid to meet the problems which arise in a changing economy and changing race relations.

The will of Miss Caroline Phelps-Stokes provided that her residual estate would go to a fund which, among other things, should be devoted to the education of the Negro. Among the first activities of this fund was the establishment of fellowships at two Southern State Universities for the study of race problems and the study of Negro private and higher schools. The other activities in the field of race relations in this country were devoted to research, counsel and cooperation with other foundations, and donations to miscellaneous strategic causes. The fund was also of tremendous value in carrying the principles which had proven sound in American education to Africa and the Near East.

Another fundamental need of Negro schools was for better facilities and equipment. Rural school buildings were in sorry straits. Only a small proportion had originally been built as schools. Many were taught in churches or abandoned cabins which had been converted to school uses. They were poorly lighted, warmed by wood stoves, and equipped with homemade, backless benches for the pupils. A very large percentage were one-teacher schools where all grades sat together and recited one at a time on one side of the room while the others tried to study.

Julius Rosenwald, President of Sears Roebuck and Company, and a trustee of Tuskegee was, on one of his visits, taken to inspect some small model buildings which had been built near Tuskegee to replace some of the hovels formerly used for schools. As a result, on his fiftieth birthday, in 1912, he decided to experiment in a modest way by aiding schools which were to be erected under the direction of Booker T. Washington. This work continued to grow successfully until 1920 when the interest of Mr. Rosenwald increased to the point that he wished to extend the work widely. He established an office for the administration of the Julius Rosenwald Fund in accordance with a specific plan, some of the provisions of which are well worth quoting: "The Fund will cooperate with public school authorities in the effort to build and equip better school houses for Negroes; sites and buildings shall be the property of public school authorities. The trustees of the Fund and the State Department of Education must agree as to the number of buildings. The site must include ample space for playgrounds and for farm work. The site and plan for the building must be approved by a representative of the Fund. It is a condition precedent to receiving aid from the Fund that the people of the community shall secure from other sources, such as public school funds or private contributions, an amount equal to or greater than that given by the Fund. The amount appropriated by the Fund shall not exceed $500 for a one-teacher school, $800 for a two-teacher school and $1,000 for a three-teacher school. (Building costs were considerably lower then than now). A teachers' home should be provided. The Fund will cooperate in erecting such homes in a limited number of selected localities."

The conditions were immediately accepted by the superintendents of schools of the Southern States and Mr. S. L. Smith, of the Tennessee State Department of Education, an expert in school construction, was put in charge. Before the close of its building operations the fund had stimulated the construction of over five thousand rural Negro schools. Upon the dedication of the five-thousandth it was stated that twenty-five million dollars had been invested in better buildings since the plan started. Of this sum the Fund had invested four million dollars; the Negroes themselves, four and a half million; and white people a million. Most of the money had come from public funds. At that time one in every five rural schools for Negroes in the South was a Rosenwald school. One-third of all rural Negro children enrolled and one-third of the teachers employed were in Rosenwald schools.

In addition to the school building program the Rosenwald Fund made valuable contributions to race relations by the promotion of research and the training of Southern leadership by means of fellowships and scholarships. The general activities of the Fund were under the direction of Edwin K. Embree and were stimulated by the live interest of Mr. Rosenwald's family.

The activities of these foundations and individuals have helped the South along the road of developing Negro education. Futhermore, in each instance, the help has been given, not as a substitute for, but as a stimulus to local effort and each dollar donated to the region has been mutiplied many times by additional public appropriations and the results have been cumulative as time passed.

The funds available to these foundations were substantial but, even so, they were small in proportion to the staggering total needed to meet the pressing requirements of Southern schools. They therefore had to be concentrated in strategic points for purposes which were recognized as sound and which would eventually be supported by the people of the South. Thus the value of their contribution was far greater than the amounts appropriated and the benefits lasted beyond the expiration of the grants.

The personal prestige of the men employed to administer these funds can hardly be measured in dollars and cents. It was universally recognized that they were wholly unselfish and wise and patient in dealing with local officials. Thus they were able to accomplish much merely by their presence.

CHAPTER 13

Separate But Still Unequal

The tradition of cooperation between the North, the South, and the Negro in educational movements was well established by the beginning of the twentieth century. A foundation of good will for public education had been laid by the pioneer work of the Conference for Education in the South, the Southern Education Board, various foundations, and Southern educators who had dedicated their lives to the cause. Most of the prejudice against public schools had been dispelled or greatly weakened. There was, however, still some grumbling about the idea of public education for Negroes. Education would only spoil a good farm worker, some said. To educate a Negro would make him want to get out of his place was believed by others. Still others thought it was unjust to tax white property holders to support Negro schools. Gradually the idea of Negro public schools was accepted, however, as public schools for white children became more firmly established.

My first full time job after leaving college in 1913 was on the staff of the Phelps-Stokes Fund. We had set ourselves the task of writing a report on all Negro private schools which solicited donations and all public schools above the elementary grades. Thus I was given the opportunity to move about the South in major cities and small towns, in plantation areas and areas of small farming. I got acquainted with the school conditions as they were and with the men who were working to improve them.

It was readily apparent that the South was carrying a heavy load on a weak back. By 1910, the Southern population, both white and Negro, was double that of 1870. The Negro population, which had to be educated from scratch, included nearly two and one-half million children of school age. The tax resources with which to build the new educational system were pitifully meager. As late as 1940 the ability of the Southern States to support education, measured by the income per school child, was only about one-half of that for the rest of the nation.

This small tax base not only had to develop an educational system but had to build other state institutions and a system of roads which could get the farmer out of the mud. It is said that a country couple came to the county courthouse for a marriage license accompanied by three or four children. Noticing that the children called them Ma and Pa, the clerk asked if they had been married before. "No," they explained, "we've been trying to get around to that but the roads were too poor to get into town to attend to it."

Above all the South was in need of funds to reequip agriculture and lay foundations for budding industry. The region was particularly handicapped in its efforts to accumulate capital since its economy was, in a way, a colonial appendage of the rest of the nation. A substantial part of its gross income was drained off for interest payments. Its staple crops were sold at world prices but its supplies were, in large measure, purchased from other regions at domestic prices including a profit for the outside producer. Freight rates were so regulated as to give low rates to raw materials going out and high rates to finished products coming back and most of the railroad profits went to stockholders elsewsere.

The Southern farmer slaved to raise cotton, shipped it to the Northern mills and bought it back in the form of cotton cloth. His shoes were made in New England, his mules raised in Missouri, his implements fabricated in the Midwest. Although richly underlain with fine granite, the South even had to call on Vermont to carve some of the Confederate monuments which stand in the courthouse squares.

Thus it was that although the foundation for the development of education had been laid, the superstructure was barely started. What I saw in moving about the back roads in the South was that in the rural districts a great majority of Negro schools were of the one-room variety. The buildings were crowded and dilapidated and drab. Such expansion as had occurred overreached the supply of trained Negro teachers. Many of the rural schools were taught by young girls who had had little more training than the pupils. It was said that they held school instead of teaching school. Their salaries were nominal, averaging in some states as low as $150 per year, hardly enough to compete with the wages of domestic servants in town. Furthermore this low salary was only paid for four or five months in the year, as that was a limit of the rural term which the budget for education would support.

Very few of the rural schools went beyond the fourth or fifth grade. In fact, with only four or five months a year of instruction it would have required ten years before a pupil would reach the level of the fifth grade as measured by normal educational standards. By then, he would be old enough to go to work.

"I never visit one of these schools," a Southern supervisor of rural schools has stated, "without feeling that we are wasting a large part of the money and we are neglecting a great opportunity. The Negro school houses are miserable beyond all description. They are usually without comfort, equipment, proper lighting or sanitation. Nearly all of the Negroes of school age in the district are crowded into the miserable structures during the short term that the school runs. Most of the teachers were absolutely untrained and have been given certificates, not because they passed the examination, but because it is necessary to have some kind of a Negro teacher. Among the Negro rural schools which I have visted, I have found only one in which the highest class knew the multiplication table."

In all the Phelps-Stokes staff visited over 700 schools, mostly private. It took nearly three years for three of us to do this. About half of the high school pupils were still being educated in private schools. Public institutions accommodated less than two-fifths of the college students—most of these being in one national university, Howard.

It was clear that Southern counties, especially the rural counties in the Black Belt, were economizing to a shocking extent by their neglect of Negro education. The Southwide annual average expenditure for teachers' salaries was $10.32 per each white child and $2.89 per each Negro child. In many Black Belt counties, Negroes were given a year's education at less than a dollar a head. The record discrepancy showed up in one Louisiana parish which spent $27.73 per white child and 47 cents per Negro child.

Many parents were keenly ambitious for their children to have educational advantages, but many were content to keep them at home much of the time to do chores, especially during the cotton-picking season when the landlord was pressing for labor. As a result, attendance was far below enrollment and many children became discouraged with the whole process and dropped out of school early. Only a fifth of the Negro pupils progressed beyond the fourth grade in 1910. Compulsory school laws had been placed on the books but there was no thought of enforcement as long as there were not enough buildings to house all the Negro children or teachers to teach them. The Negro got only the crumbs from a poor man's table.

It is extremely unfortunate that, at this time of great need, there should have been a sharp and bitter division in the ranks of the Negroes and of the supporters of Negro education as to the type of education which was best for the race. The split went much deeper than a disagreement over educational policy and extended to the whole philosophy of race relations.

The conservative wing was led by Booker T. Washington, who was exceptionally successful in reconciling the aspirations of the Negro with Southern white caution. The result was a policy of conciliation and gradualism reluctantly accepting, for the moment, segregation and disfranchisement as the price for winning economic and educational concessions from the conservatives of the South. "Let down your buckets where you are" was the slogan for achieving economic and material progress. The corresponding educational policy was one of agricultural and industrial training with emphasis on thoroughness and character building. The chief concern was for elementary and high school education for the masses recognizing at the same time that higher education was necessary for training leaders.

The idealistic wing had as its principal spokesman W. E. B. DuBois who, in 1905, began to agitate for full citizenship rights as an immediate rather than a distant goal. Du Bois organized the Niagra Movement which, in 1910, merged with the National Association for the Advancement of Colored People as the vehicle for his movement. He was a brilliant writer but one whose pen was often dipped in vinegar and whose sarcasm was so sharp as to alienate Southern opinion rather than to win it over. His followers were impatient with industrial and agricultural training, looking upon it as a device for keeping the Negro in a subordinate status. Their emphasis was almost exclusively on education of college and professional grade and their strategy was that of constant agitation and pressure to force concessions in segregation and disfrancisement.   After a trip through the South, Ray Stannard Baker commented that such vitriolic rivalry could hardly be understood unless observed firsthand. The controversy was particularly unfortunate in that it confused the minds of the rank and file of Negroes as to just which direction they should follow.

A sober appraisal of the situation as it actually was would have made it clear that both types of approach to race progress were necessary and not mutually antagonistic except as they were artificially alleged to be. Before colleges could expand there had to be a sufficient annual output of high school graduates to fill their freshman classes and these needed to be well grounded in fundamentals. Progress demanded more and more professional and business men to set examples, but for every one of these dozens needed to be trained to meet the needs for elementary teachers, skilled tradesmen, and farmers.

The controversy as to the optimum type of education has now faded but the disagreement as to the best method of solving race differences continues and probably will continue for years to come.

In spite of all handicaps, however, public education began to advance slowly. As white schools began to improve, Negro schools reaped some of the advantages. The increase in taxable wealth, insistence of Negro leaders on fairer treatment, the stimulation of foundations, and the stirring of the public conscience promoted slow progress.

Going to the superintendent of schools of the Louisiana parish in which our Phelps-Stokes study revealed the widest discrepancy between per capita expenditure for white and Negro children, B. C. Caldwell, the field agent of the Jeanes Fund, asked; "Do you know according to this publication of the U.S. Bureau of Education your parish has broken a record and leads the whole United States?" Anticipating a pat on the back the superintendent asked, "What record, what for?" Caldwell replied: "For robbing the Negro." This shock treatment was effective and the superintendent, being a man with a conscience, wanted to know what could be done about it. Caldwell suggested, as a starter, the employment of a Jeanes supervising teacher to raise standards of instruction and the erection of one or two Rosenwald buildings to improve facilities. The superintendent pursuaded his board to go along and the parish began to find the road to progress.

This scene, with less dramatics, was repeated over and over in the hundreds of visits of state supervisors of Negro schools to school officials. Slowly but surely their influences permeated the South. Following the example of their leaders, the Negroes themselves exerted more pressure for better advantages and the Southern people generally began to feel more responsibility for improving the opportunities of their fellow citizens. Progress, however, was painfully slow at first. All during the bollweevil period and the great depression the South was still short of cash for public improvements. It was not until the boom following World War II brought widespread prosperity that rapid progress was made. The middle years of this century, however, have witnessed some phenomenal advances.

In 1955 about 90 per cent of the Negro children were enrolled in school and illiteracy had almost disappeared except in the older generation. The Negro had become thoroughly inoculated with the American zeal for education as the key to advancement. The school term for practically all Negro schools has been lengthened to nine months. The most spectacular advance, however, came in the salaries paid to Negro teachers. In the twelve years following 1940 their wages in comparable dollars more than doubled. Waking up to the poor condition of Negro school buildings, the South has invested millions of dollars in Negro public school plant and equipment. Since some of these Negro schools have been the most recently constructed they are more modern than the white schools. Between 1940 and 1952 the per pupil value of buildings and equipment for white children increased over 100%, while the amount for Negro children increased nearly 300%. Even with this advance, however, the per pupil value for Negroes was still less than for white. This also was partly due to the smaller proportion of Negroes who were enrolled in high school.

Negro high-school enrollment, especially, had skyrocketed from 33,000 in 1920 to nearly 400,000, of whom over 50,000 a year graduate. In other words, there are now more high school graduates from public high schools alone each year than there were students in 1920. No longer does the Negro have to lean so heavily on mission schools for high school opportunity.

In the middle 1950's, Negro colleges enrolled over 75,000 full-time regular students, about half in publicly supported institutions. This takes no account of the numerous students in the nonsegregated institutions. But the Negro population was still under-represented in higher education since they enrolled only 3 per cent of the Nation's college students. The annual educational income of the 104 separate Negro colleges was nearly 50 million dollars of which over half was from Southern state treasuries.

Since teacher's salaries make up the bulk of public school expenditures and teaching efficiency is the most important element in the quality of training, the most significant trend toward equalization is to be found in this respect. In recent years most Southern States have adopted uniform scales for teacher's salaries which are applicable to both races—the variations depending on the level of training and length of service. This has resulted in two states in a statewide average salary for Negro teachers slightly larger than that for white teachers because the Negroes have remained in the profession longer and have taken advantage of advanced training opportunities. Since the proportion of Negro pupils in high school was smaller in most states, the proportion of high-paid Negro high school teachers reduced their average somewhat. By 1952 the Southwide average annual salary for white teachers was about three thousand dollars and for Negroes was just under twenty-six hundred. Much of this divergence was attributable to lower salaries in Mississippi where the pay for Negroes was ony about half that for whites.

There is still a tendency in the Black Belt counties to crowd more Negroes into each class room and hire fewer Negro teachers, less is also spent on transportation, school lunches and other services for Negroes, thus reducing the expenditure per pupil. By this measure, in 1952, $115 was expended on each Negro pupil and $190 on each white pupil.

The widest gap still remained in the provision of college education. Most Southern States not only maintain a university for white students but also technical schools, womens' colleges, and teacher training institutions. On the other hand, there are, for Negroes, only 22 state schools of collegiate grade. Of these 17 are land-grant colleges which receive federal subsidies. In the 17 states which maintained separate schools, only about an eighth of the annual state appropriations for higher education went to Negro schools and about the same proportion had been invested in buildings and equipment of Negro colleges, although Negroes constitute over a fifth of the population. Again, however, we must be reminded that they drop out of school faster than whites and so are not yet fully prepared for equal facilities at the higher level. Another serious discrepancy is in facilities for graduate training. Until recently opportunities for training at this level were drastically limited in the South, with the result that the majority of Negroes who wished to advance their professional career have had to study in other regions. The Southern States have, after a fashion, tried to rectify this neglect by providing out-of-state scholarships for qualified graduate students.

Such attempts to measure equality by statistical averages are beset by many pitfalls. Rural schools are not so well supported as city schools. Rich counties contribute more liberally than poor counties. Educational opportunity, therefore, was to a large degree dependent upon where a child happened to live. Without doubt a considerable part of the advance of Negro education was brought about by the movement to the city. Likewise some of the apparent narrowing of the gap was caused by the fact that the proportion of Negroes in cities became nearer to that of the whites.

After allowing for these population shifts, however, even a superficial examination of the figures will show that, in the 1940's, when the South really began to participate in national prosperity, they showed a remarkable willingness to attempt to equalize the education of the races. After ninety years of slow progress the rate became almost phenomenal.

But this surge to progress was not entirely spontaneous on the part of the South. Constant pressures, litigation, and threats of litigation by the National Association for the Advancement of Colored People were necessary to get things started, especially in the equalization of teachers' salaries and of the opportunities for college education.

All this time the white public schools were also forging ahead in the effort to keep pace with the rest of the nation, with the result that the gap between the educational opportunity of the two races narrowed but slowly, the most rapid closing beginning after 1945.

In spite of the discrepancies in educational provision for the two races in the early 1950's recent progress had been so rapid that the concensus of informed opinion was that, given another 10 years the South would have made good on its commitment to equalize educational opportunity for Negroes. They were beginning to show genuine pride in their progress and willingness to push farther but they were not to be given another 10 years. The Supreme Court ruled that true equality cannot be obtained in separate facilities because the enforced separation affixes a badge of inferiority and destroys some of the incentive to learn. This decision divided the two races into hostile camps. The white people of the Deep South are determined to cling to their separate schools as long as possible and the Negroes feel equally as strongly that they, with the backing of the courts can force a relaxation

CHAPTER 15

Segregation: Voluntary and Involuntary

Segregation was also a part of the racial pattern in which I grew up. The etiquette of race contact was complex and at times confusing. It was not based on natural reactions but had to be learned like the alphabet or the multiplication tables.

Southerners, white and colored, are traditionally friendly, cordial, and hospitable people. Friendliness and cordiality between the races were strong but the outward expression between white and black followed a different code from the one dictated by good manners among white people. Often, when a white man greeted a colored man on the street the genuineness of their affection was manifest from the tones of their voices but they seldom shook hands. The Negro was addressed by his first name, but if the acquaintance was slight, the white man was always Mr. Smith or Mr. Jones. If the two were old friends the Negro used the white man's first name but always with a prefix. It was always "Mr. John" or "Cap'n John." That is the way it had been for generations.

As a very young child, I could play on Uncle Harvie's plantation with the colored children but after 8 or 10 years of age it was rarely done. To call a white playmate "nigger" was a form of profanity and invited a fight. Negroes also objected to being called "nigger" or "black" as the words usually carried a derogatory meaning. It is said that a Negro was once hauled into court for fighting. When he explained to the judge that he had been called a black rascal, he asked, "Judge what would you do if somebody called you that?" The judge replied that no one would think of calling him a black rascal. "Well Judge," asked the defendant, "suppose somebody called you the kind of rascal that you is?"

One of my childhood treats was to ride on the streetcar to the park. We were always accompanied by a Negro nurse and everyone understood that she would sit in the white section of the car with us. There was no way around it. We were too young to be unattended and for us to have gone into the Negro section with her would have been unthinkable.

We ate food prepared by Negro servants but did not eat with

them. This rule was capable of exceptions. As young men, when meal time overtook us while hunting or fishing, it was permissable to stop by the house of Negro acquaintances and offer to share the game with them if they would prepare some for us. Sometimes we ate together, sometimes they saved their share, but it was eaten from their table and their dishes.

John Henry Grice was a strong influence in my boyhood. He was the general factotum at the Y. M. C. A. He was essentially a good man and he was also a skilled, self-taught, masseur. His big gentle hands could work magic with a kinked or bruised muscle. He was a good cook. He demonstrated his ability each summer at our camps but after entertaining us with folk songs in the evening he retired to his own tent. Although we boys weighed his advice as carefully as we did that of Mr. Forbes, the Y. M. C. A. Secretary, Mr. Forbes was always Mr. Forbes and John Henry was just John Henry, never Mr. Grice.

Later I heard big boys talk of what the young white men and colored girls did at night and often wondered what their mode of address was or how they felt if they happened to meet on the street next day.

The results of their youthful misconduct were all too evident to the casual observer who could not help noting the large number of bronze and olive skinned people who bore a strong family resemblance to many of the old, aristocratic families. The old families were interrelated in complex ways but the family tree was never traced across the color line.

When I thought of segregation at all it was most bewildering. Afterwards, when I began to read and hear what intelligent Negroes thought about it, I realized that they must have a difficult time finding their way through the maze of color etiquette. For the white man it was not so difficult. He could offer to shake hands with a Negro acquaintance but the Negro could not risk the initiative. If the white man sat in the wrong section of a streetcar he might be corrected or considered absentminded but for a Negro to violate the code might bring down on him a rude rebuke, the loss of his job, or even rough handling.

The unwritten code of social etiquette was likely to vary from place to place in an unpredictable manner. Booker T. Washington, who was able to laugh even when the joke was on him, had the habit of making good will tours through the South and discussing his philosophy of race relations before mixed audiences.

He told of the time when he was scheduled to speak in a small Flordia city. The only place in town large enough to hold the crowd was the courthouse. When this was announced the sentiment of the town was sharply divided. Part of the people thought it was all right for a Negro to make a speech in the courthouse, the others thought he should be there only as a defendant. The meeting was held, however, and he, with his usual diplomacy, won over the crowd. After the meeting a very drunk man came up to him and said "Booker Washington, you are a great man. I was against your speaking in the courthouse, but now I know I was wrong. You are the greatest man in the country". "Well", said Washington—"That covers a lot of territory, how about Theodore Roosevelt (who was then President)?" The drunk said, "I used to think that T. R. was the greatest man in the country until he invited you to lunch".

New situations called for new inventions in the field of segregation. When Atlanta's first skyscraper, the Candler Building, was built, a bank of elevators was installed. All but one elevator were marked "for white only" and that one was for colored. In effect, the "colored" elevator became a mixed elevator because if a white man was in a hurry and the Negro elevator was about to go up he would get on.

A near serious outbreak occurred in the old Atlanta Union Station. The architect had provided only three gates for entering and leaving the trains. As a matter of convenience whites and Negroes went out through the same gate so that tickets could be punched by one man, but upon alighting from a train they were supposed to come out through separate gates. One Negro, not understanding the situation, thought that since he had left through the same gate with white people he should come back with them. He started out through the white gate and an attendant began to push him back. The Negro, not knowing what was happening, bent his umbrella over the attendant's head. Only the work of very cool heads prevented a small riot. This illustrates one of the features of segregation most irritating to Negroes. Namely that those charged with its administration were largely low-paid white employees who were none too considerate in dealing with the situation.

These customs were what Major Moton called gravels in the shoe of the Negro and it is very uncomfortable to walk constantly on gravel. But, Jim Crow in the form of statues governing public contacts, was relatively a newcomer on the Southern scene at the beginning of this century. It will surprise those who believe that segregation is and always was the Southern way of life to learn that the rigid segregation of the races by law as we know it today was not written on the statute books until the decade of the 1890's. The exceptions were separate school and separate army units.

The Jim Crow statutes came at about the same time as the withdrawal of the vote in the decade which was characterized by the surrender to hate and passion. In fact, the two issues were bound up together by the demagogs and the wavers of the red shirts. Up to that time there has been relatively free association of the races in public facilities.

For several years after the Civil War the South was subjected to a number of inspection tours by ex-abolitionists who wanted to assure themselves that their will was being done. The reports from several of these are quoted by Woodward in his *Strange Career of Jim Crow*. These reports were in agreement as to the surprising lack of discrimination or friction between the races in their contacts on trains, restaurants, other refreshment places, street cars, and all public facilities. Some compared these customs with conditions in New England and came to the conclusion that on the whole New England was not doing so well. These observations were confirmed by an English Radical Member of Parliament who reported that he was somewhat taken aback to find relationship so much freer than he had expected.

How much of this freedom of contact was due to the Federal Civil Rights Law is not readily discernible, but it is significant that this law was abrogated in 1883 and that there was still a period of a decade and a half before the legal vise of segregation began to be tightened and the tightening came after the bitter political struggle between the radical and conservative elements in Southern politics.

Nor were these segregation laws enacted without Southern opposition. In 1897 a Charleston, South Carolina, editor commented on the proposed Jim Crow law for trains: "We can do nothing whatever about Northern or outside opinion in the matter. It is a question for our own decision according to our own ideas as to what is right and expedient, and our opinion is that we have no more need for a Jim Crow system this year than we had last year and a great deal less than we had twenty or thirty years ago. Such a law would be unnecessary and uncalled for, a needless affront to our respectable and well behaved colored people." Before that a Southern editor had written: "It is a great deal pleasanter to travel with respectable and well behaved colored people than with unmannerly and ruffianly white men."

But the voices of moderation were drowned out by the chorus of race haters and fanatics. Within a few years a network of segregation laws was spread like an epidemic through the states and cities prohibiting the contact of the races in every phase of public life.

An iron curtain was inexorably fixed between the races. They could work together and joke together on the street but otherwise when the Negro appeared in public he must retire behind the barriers—quarantined as a leper. To the white man the curtain was a symbol of superiority by which the most lowly member of the dominant race could console himself with the feeling that he was superior to somebody. To the Negro it was a badge of hate, a symbol of shame and a device which made him prey to the most flagrant discrimination, a method of assuring him that he could not participate equally in the progress which he was helping to achieve, that he could never be a full-fledged citizen.

Segregation is a general term covering any degree of separateness of the races. There are, however, at least three types of segregation which arise from different circumstances and different motives. The first type, which arises from geographic or economic differences, might better be termed isolation. The second, which arises from the trait of human nature which makes like seek to associate with like, might well be called voluntary clannishness or solidarity. The third, which, by law or custom, decrees separate facilities for the receipt of any service to which a person should be entitled as an American citizen or by reason of the payment of a fixed fee, can be considered as forcible division.

The three are often confused in argument. Frequently all types of segregation are branded as immoral, un-Christian, and un-American, when, as a matter of fact, the accuser has only one type in mind. Just as frequently all segregation is defended as inevitable and necessary to racial harmony and to the preservation of white standards when, in reality, the argument of the defender applies only to certain types of separation. There might be considerably more light and less heat on the subject if the discussants could keep in mind just what is biting them when they froth at the mouth about segregation.

Geographic or economic isolation comes through the impersonal operation of the economic system. In the rural South certain lands, particularly adapted to the culture of cotton and tobacco, have attracted and held Negro labor to a greater extent than others. There was a cleavage between the counties surrounding my home city, Athens. To the north, in the Upper Piedmont hills, Negro populations were distinctly in the minority. To the South, the better cotton lands had been held in larger tracts and cultivated with Negro labor. These were the Black Belt counties which still have heavy Negro majorities. Within the Black Belt counties further concentration was occuring. The white farmers were moving to town faster, leaving the rural areas blacker. When it is considered that the average plantation had about 16 tenant families with one white landlord, if he lived on the place, it will be realized that six such plantations side by side would include 100 Negro families and a maximum of six white families, constituting a fairly solid Negro settlement covering some ten square miles.

The process in the city was somewhat similar. Negroes wanted to live near their work in houses which they could afford with their meagre wages. Houses were built for them in areas where low-priced land could be bought thus resulting in a high degree of concentration. In my home town, Athens, Georgia, there were twelve distinct Negro settlements scattered through a small city. The core of these settlements was solid but the fringes often contained mixed blocks. Here and there servants houses still remained in the back yards of employers in exclusive neighborhoods which was the traditional antebellum pattern.

The evolution of the Negro neighborhood in the large Northern city, which in many instances resulted in more compact settlement than in Southern cities, was a somewhat different process since the Negro here was rapidly filling up areas previously occupied by white people. The influence of economic forces and social cohesion were, however, equally traceable.

Once the Negro neighborhood was staked out by the economic forces, it was solidified and extended by the second urge to separateness arising from the desire of like to associate with like. The economic neighborhood tended to become the social community.

The value placed on this sociability is illustrated by the philosophy of the yard man who was employed by one of my friends.

When she sympathized with him about the disadvantaged position of the Negroes and their run-down neighborhoods, he replied: "Don't you worry too much about us, Miss Aline. You ought to be a Negro just once on Saturday night".

Each city has a pattern of its own, the degree of separateness depending upon topography, the distribution of industry, the layout of transportation lines, and the historical trends of property values. The city neighborhood was something into which the growing Negro population had to fit itself as best it could without much individual choice. From time to time shortlived attempts have been made to chrystallize residential segregation in both rural and urban communities by law, but these soon proved unconstitutional, impractical, and to a large extent unnecessary since economic realities, social cohesion and community pressures were sufficient.

Although these neighborhoods arise from the operation of economic and social forces, their existence opens the door to discrimination and exploitation. It is easy for the municipal authorities to neglect them. They are served by the poorest streets in town, sewer and water facilities are lacking, and sanitary inspection lax. Discrimination against them is more evident in cities in which the Negro is unable to protect himself with the ballot. Even so it is practically impossible to determine where economic disadvantage leaves off and discrimination begins since the low property values in such neighborhoods will not support the assessments for all municipal improvements.

The point at which separate neighborhoods become objectionable to the educated and respectable colored people is when law or community pressure locks them in with the unkempt and unmannerly members of their own race.

The second type of segregation, the association of like with like, or solidarity, needs no sanction of law nor can it be changed by law. It is a matter of personal choice. Lord Bryce observed: "As regards social relations, law can do but little save in the way of expressing the view the State takes of how its members should behave to one another. Good feeling and good manners cannot be imposed by statute." Nor is it particularly undemocratic or immoral to wish to control the choice of those whom you will invite into your home or your club or with whom you wish your children to play.

When confronted with the argument that all segregation should be abolished, it is this type of social separation which is uppermost in the Southerner's mind. The prospect of not being able to choose his own associates makes him see red and ask: "Would you like for your daughter to marry a Negro?"

Negroes themselves wish to exercise the same prerogative of choice. It is this feeling on the part of the educated Negro which understandably is back of his objection to being tied by law or custom to the disadvantaged members of his own race. A peculiar twist of the operation of exclusiveness was, until recently, observable in Charleston where there was a "high yellow" church whose members were well to do mulattoes and where black Negroes were not welcomed.

The South did not invent this type of exclusiveness nor does it have a monopoly on it. It is of the same stripe as the former attitude of steel cities to the "hunkies" or of Boston, first to the Irish then to the Italians. In fact the blue blooded Bostonian is reputed to feel that way about any one whose ancestors have not lived for generations in New England. Slavery has been blamed for the unwillingness of the white South to associate with Negroes but the etiquette of slavery was based on the customs of the English manorial system which was characterized by a rigid code of relationship between the lord of the manor and his servants or tenants. This code has its survivals in the customs of British colonials who live in lands alongside of other races. In its most extreme form it is manifest in the caste system of India (which country incidentally is one of the shrillest critics of Southern race relations) where iron clad rules govern the association between the multitudes of castes; where castes may not intermarry; where they are confined to the traditional caste occupation; and where in some cases contact with other castes is limited by restrictions on touching, associating with, dining with, or eating food cooked by outsiders. It is found in Russia in the attitude of the Russian people toward some of the ill-starred minorities of the Soviet Union.

These are only samples of the multitude of bi-racial and bi-national situations in which groups value their social solidarity.

To point out the prevalence of voluntary separation of people of different races should not imply either praise or condemnation of this practice. After all, as Lord Bryce said, that is a matter of individual morals and manners.

Social relationships are in the realm of behaviour wl good will and good manners, accomodations will be mad minimum of embarrassment. I have seen it work out meetings in the South where no separate seating was p_____. A Negro would walk in, hesitate, and look around for a seat next to another Negro. A white man would walk in and if he objected to sitting near a Negro he would sit elsewhere. If he didn't object he would sit in any seat which suited him. I have even seen it work the same way when Negro members of organizations were invited to official dinners in the South. I have seen it work that way in the unsegregated Government cafeterias in Washington for fifteen years and none of the color has ever rubbed off on me yet. Individual choice usually takes care of everybody's feelings except those of the extremely prejudiced persons who object to eating under the same roof with a person of color. There is nothing social about public contact, nor does it in any way change a person's choice as to whom he will invite into his home or seek out as a companion for wining and dining. The atmosphere could be cleared considerably if advocates of segregation could realize that public contact does not necessitate private association. It is something separate and apart from "social equality" or inter-marriage. We noted that for three decades there was little forced segregation in public facilities in the South but no social inter-mingling ensued, nor was intermarriage even thought of. There has been less enforced public segregation in the North, nor is in-termarriage a problem of consequence there.

In his calmer moments the Southern white man knows that the nine Justices of the Supreme Court are not going to march South at the head of the army to compel him to invite a Negro to dinner three nights a week, or arrange a shotgun interracial marriage for his daughter even though he may talk like he believes it when excited.

In all seriousness, however, the Southern white man feels that he has a real job on his hands to preserve the cultural standards which his ancestors have painfully evolved over centuries of time. This is especially true in areas of heavy Negro majorities where the Negroes have progressed least. A casual observer of these communities cannot fail to note that in spite of marked progress, there still exist wide differences between the average individuals of the two races in health, morals, manners and education—differences freely admitted by the most violent opponents of segregation. As long as wide differences exist the white man will put as much social distance as possible between his family and the family of the Negro.

With respect to the preservation of standards against the contacts with persons of different manners and morals, however, the white South finds itself in a quandary. Segregation is the method adopted yet the longer that the Negroes are kept apart from the currents of progress with inferior facilities, the longer will their standards be lower than those of the whites. Even in spite of these handicaps, however, an increasing number of colored people, by dint of great effort, have overcome the handicaps of their enviroment and by any measure applied, meet the requirements of first class American citizens.

Having endeavored to analyze the nature of economic and social solidarity or exclusiveness, we may summarize these by saying that these aspects of race contacts are untouchable by law and are in the realm of individual income, manners, and morals. As long as no compulsion is invoked and as long as discrimination is avoided the economic and social relationships can be worked out between men of good will and of good manners, especially when the long processes of education can be relied on to minimize gradually the repugnant differences.

When, however, the question of legal segregation in public facilities is considered, different moral principles and democratic concepts are involved. Public contacts are either in those facilities for which a Negro pays the same money as a white man and hence should receive the same service, chiefly on trains, buses, restaurants, and theatres; or they are in those institutions which administer a public service to which citizens are entitled as citizens and which a modern democracy considers necessary to develop the human values essential to the advance of civilization. Separation in this realm is Jim Crow. He writes his edicts on statute books and over doorways of separate waiting rooms and seating accommodations. He builds them into separate buildings. Everywhere he rubs it in to the Negro that he is not wanted. He labels him a second-class citizen. He pins the black badge of inferiority on all Negroes, not on the basis of economic ability, health, behaviour, or educational attainment but simply on the basis of the color of his skin. He separates all people of color from the main stream of progress, robbing them of any hope of recognition on the basis of individual achievement.

The validity of Jim Crow has, for decades, been argued from various angles, and at great length before the Supreme Court. The august body, despite the sex of the justices has reserved the right to change its mind as society changes. Jim Crow raises such legal questions as: Which rights are guaranteed to citizens by the constitution of the United States and which are derived from their citizenship in the several states and local communities? When is the denial of a right attributable to race or color and when to some other status of the individual? How do we measure equality in the protection of the law? He raises equally as pressing moral questions.

I was three years of age when the Supreme Court ruling in the case of Plessy vs. Ferguson laid down the "separate but equal" doctrine much to the satisfaction of the South. Thus, just as the demagogs were beginning to press for state Jim Crow laws, the Supreme Court stamped them with its approval *provided there was no discrimination.* For fifty years of my life that was the formula that theoretically regulated the provision of public facilities. Even as late as 1938 the Court, in its ruling on the Gaines case, held that when a state could not provide equal higher education facilities for Negroes within the state it must admit them to a regular state university thus holding to the separate but equal principle.

This was the philosophy of Henry Grady; Booker T. Washington fell for it, and summed it up in his "as separate as the fingers but as united as the hand". I discussed this years ago with Washington and no one was more aware than he of the glaring inequality of opportunities for Negroes at the time. He was, however, pinning his faith to the honesty and fairness of the Southerner to eliminate dicrimination as rapidly as possible.

In effect the South, at that time, made a bargain with the Negro and the rest of the nation which, if written down, would have read something like this: Let us keep our white institutions separate and we will see to it that your Negro institutions are equally as good. However, this bargain has not been kept. On the question of giving the Negro equality in the schools the South is somewhat in the position of the colored man who was suing for divorce and alleged that his wife was always demanding money. He said: "It is always money, money, money". Upon being asked what she did with all this money he said: "I don't know. I never have given her any."

Strongly extenuating circumstances have been pleaded by the South but, as convincing as they might seem, they do not make the Negro happy about being Jim Crowed and discriminated against. The wishful thinking of some Southerners who assert that "our Negroes are satisfied unless they are stirred up by agitators" is far from the truth.

What is really stirring them up is that they are deeply disturbed and disappointed by their own constant observation of the numerous good things of democracy which are labeled "for white people only."

In very recent years the South has made heroic efforts to wipe out discrimination, but the gap had become too wide to close quickly. Although the extent to which equality in schools had been achieved by 1950 (discussed earlier in Chapter 13) was considerable, what the Supreme Court's 1954 decision in this connection seemed to imply was that because nearly 100 years had elapsed since the surrender at Appomattox without the South succeeding in living up to the separate but equal formula, it was time to change the rule to 'equal must be identical.' Furthermore the opinion seemed to imply that separate facilities could never be equal for the reason that enforced separation affixes a badge of inferiority which imposes a mental roadblock against the best effort.

It is doubtful whether Southern leaders realized the staggering financial commitment which they made by pledging equality of school facilities. The schools of the wealthier regions were ahead of the white schools of the South and the Southern white schools were far superior to those of the Negro and all three of them were constantly lifting their standards. Thus educational progress became a three way race with the Southern white schools trying to approximate the standards of other regions and at the same time trying to bring the Negro schools closer to the same level.

The first dent which was made in the segregation wall in the Deep South was in public transportation. Rulings of the Supreme Court first opened pullman accommodations, then railway accommodations to Negro interstate travelers. Local day coaches and bus service have remained separate until recently. This change in interstate travel was accomplished without too much friction because there were very few Negroes in the South who too terstate trips and these had to be sufficiently well up in nomic scale to afford to pay for first class travel. Seldom wer more than one or two on a trip. The white man who obj often had the opportunity of changing his reservation. The ductor always arranged, if possible, to put the Negro passengers in separate sections. In the still newer mode of air travel much of which is interstate, no segregation has appeared. The Southern airports have no separate waiting rooms for the two races and the few Negroes who have enough money to afford air travel are seldom noticed.

The question of desegregation of schools, however, is entirely different and much more difficult. There is an element of compulsion in the pressure to desegregate schools which is absent from other steps toward integration. This compulsion comes about because all the States have compulsory education laws. The way the South looks at it is that if the state compels all children to go to school and the Supreme Court compels the integration of races in the schools the white children will in effect be forced to attend mixed schools.

The consideration which makes it particularly difficult for the conservative Southerner to accept the enforced mixture in the schools is that this is something which his children are forced to do and many parents who would accept desegregation for themselves are reluctant to see it imposed on their children, particularly since the school is an extension of the family and in many respects has taken over the functions of the parents.

Up to this point the discussion of segregation has, for the most part, been in terms of abstract principles. The problem cannot be dismissed, however, without consideration of the practical difficulty in which the people of varying shades of opinion in the Deep South find themselves in the effort to reconcile their views with those of the rest of the nation. In this connection I have in the past year followed the press and interviewed as many informed people as possible to probe Southern public opinion on the subject of the desegregation decisions of the Supreme Court as they relate to public facilities.

We are considering a region where men still say that this generation has been cursed by the errors of its ancestors who, along with New England neighbors, brought the black man to these shores, saddling the region with a bi-racial population which mingled two races of widely different cultures, and which evolved undemocratic types of economic and social relationships. They feel that they of the tenth generation are still paying for the mistakes of the past and that, of late, they have been expected to pay up rather suddenly. No less do the Negroes feel that they are paying heavily for events in which they had no choice.

Here and there in the region, however, men will say that these errors of the past offer the people of the South the challenging opportunity to prove that democracy can be made to work even under the most adverse circumstances.

Up to 1930, the South as a whole was the home of over nine-tenths of the Negroes and the seven old plantation states of the Southeast included over 50%. These States, in which the proportions of the races are nearer equal are also the ones in which the least progress has been made in bringing up the standard of living of the Negro and where consequently adjustments are the most difficult. They are Virginia, North Carolina, South Carolina, Georgia, Alabama, Mississippi and Louisiana. They feel that if the conscience of the Nation gets aroused about once every 100 years over the fact that the status of the Negro is a national concern they are entitled to some consideration by reason of the fact that during the other 99 years they have had to carry the major responsibility.

They are outspoken in their genuine pride in such progress as they have been able to make and startled and chagrined to be suddenly told not only that their progress has been too slow but that it has been achieved under erroneous principles. They feel somewhat like a man who is playing a game only to have the rules changed suddenly by outsiders.

As of 1954 there is no longer a solid South. The differences between the Upper South and the Deep South (Florida being more similar to the upper South) began to appear in the reaction to the decisions abrogating disfranchisement but became clear after the ruling against segregation in the schools. All but seven of the States which formerly had legal segregation in their schools have gone along with the ruling of the Supreme Court at least to the extent of removing State laws prohibiting mixed schools even though this action has been repugnant to many of their citizens. These states are in the Upper South where the proportion of Negroes in the population is smaller and where the situation is not so difficult as in the Black Belts.

Four large border cities, Baltimore, Washington, D.C., Louisville, and St. Louis, had abolished segregated schools by September 1956. Likewise schools opened in 1956 in some 780 smaller communities with varying degrees of desegregation.

Very little of the predicted race friction has occured in these places. In only four of these mixed situations did violence threaten and in these four prompt action by the local officials brought the situation under control. In some of these communities opposition seems to have been based on ignorance of the true situation which was exaggerated by professional agitators. Some of the trouble-makers thought that something was being put over on them by the local school officials and were unaware that they were defying a ruling of the Supreme Court. This is a clear demonstration of the need for careful planning and preparation of public opinion before integration actually begins.

Problems of educational administration did, however, arise. Vexing questions of school health, extra-classroom activities, discipline, teacher assignment, and difference in level of pupil achievment have plagued the school boards, but nowhere have these problems seemed insoluable given time and good will.

The removal of state prohibitions against mixed schools does not mean that desegregation takes place immediately in every school. Some communities are slow to act unless prodded. What actually takes place when legal barriers are removed is that the geography of residential distribution dictates that some schools will remain all white, some all Negro, and some, particularly the high schools, will be mixed.

As a matter of fact the 780 odd communities with some degree of desegregation include only about one-eighth of the total Negro school population. Thus, even in the Border States the process spreads slowly and in the Deep South will spread even more slowly. There is, however, historic precedent in the North for this slowness. It required 30 years of agitation topped off by 10 years of active litigation before the public schools of Boston were desegregated in 1855. Separate schools remained the practice in several Northern States long after the Civil War and here also protracted litigation was necessary before the opposition of the public could be overcome. In short, many Northerners, ignorant of their own history seem to expect the Deep South to do overnight what they required years to do in a simpler situation.

In 1956 I visited several of the seven stubborn Deep South States which were violently opposed to any integration. Even here, however, it was apparent that sentiment varied from community to community despite the seemingly solid front presented by the state politicians. One county in Virginia and several in North Carolina had taken steps looking toward desegregation only to be slapped down so hard by state officials that others would not even admit that they had entertained such an idea.

Both Virginia and North Carolina had passed acts which were voted for on the assumption that they enabled local communities to exercise their descretion as to the steps to be taken to comply with the decision of the Supreme Court. But the state politicians cynically demonstrated that they did not mean that, for no sooner did a county attempt to follow its own inclinations than it was subjected to the pressure from the state department of education or the legislature to cease and desist. Some states anticipated any local initiative by passing laws which would withhold state school funds from any county in which Negroes were admitted to mixed schools. In short, the very states which have yelled loudest for state rights vs. federal interference have demonstrated the greatest reluctance to recognize county rights against state interference. Thus there is in these states a false front of solidarity erected and defended by state officials. This came about partially because of the unfortunate timing of the decision of the Court which was handed down during the heat of state political campaigns, giving the successful candidates the opportunity to thump their chests and vow that there would be no mixture in the schools as long as they were in office. It also gave them the opportunity to inflame the emotions of the people before they had had the chance to consider their problem calmly. Subsequent campaigns have demonstrated that feelings continued to run so strong that the race issue has defeated some very popular candidates. At least for some years, therefore, it would appear that no constructive action is to be expected from politicians.

The opinion which was unanimously held by all those that I interviewed in 1956 was that desegregation of the schools was certain to come eventually. The only variation of opinion was on the questions of how and how soon the goal could be reached.

Some thought that reasonable progress might be made in a year or two and others felt that the deep South might temporize for another hundred years.

Thus the stubborn seven states are in the position of a man who knows that he must swim a cold river. He knows that it is going to be unpleasant but the longer he shivers on the bank and imagines how cold it will be the more difficult it is to get started. Furthermore, never having had mixed schools, he feels that he doesn't know how to swim in this river and will have to learn as he goes along. He is afraid that he may drown in the attempt.

Some indication of how the Deep South intends to try to swim is contained in the 1956 report of the North Carolina Advisory Committee on Education—one of the most restrained statements of the position of the region:

"We are in a very dangerous situation. It could become a dreadful situation quickly. The steady and healthy progress which we have been making for more than half a century in the betterment of our racial relations has been suddenly stopped. Now the tide is running the other way. Racial tensions are mounting in North Carolina every day . . .

"We are of the unanimous opinion that the people of North Carolina will not support mixed schools. This is to say that we believe if the schools were integrated in this State, the General Assembly, representing the people, would withhold support to a degree that the result would certainly be the ruin and eventual abandonment of the public schools. Whether a particular viewpoint finds this conclusion to be good or bad, pleasant or unpleasant, it remains our conclusion and we state it as such. . . .

"We sometimes lose sight of the fact that the system of which we speak is inherently a segregated system. It could not have so developed, except as a segregated system. That should always be kept in mind. If we would 'preserve our school system' we would have to preserve a segregated system.

"The decisions of the Supreme Court of the United States have destroyed our foundation of segregation required by law. The Supreme Court has declared that the principle upon which our system was built and upon which it has rested, is no longer valid. So, we do not have the problem of 'preserving our school system.' The Supreme Court of the United States destroyed the school system which we had developed—a segregated-by-law system. Our

problem is, rather, to build a new system out of the Supreme
Court's wreckage of the old. This fact governs our whole approach
to the problem. The task which faces us is how to use what we
have left of our old educational system to provide an education
for all of the children in North Carolina.

"The decision of the Supreme Court of the United States,
however much we dislike it, is the declared law and is binding
upon us. We think that the decision was erroneous; that it was a
reversal of established law upon an unprecedented base of psychology and sociology; that it could cause more harm within the
United States than anything which has happened in fifty years.
But we must in honesty recognize that, because the Supreme
Court is the court of last resort in this country, what it has said
must stand until there is a correcting constitutional amendment
or until the Court corrects its own error. We must live and act
now under the decision of that Court. We should not delude ourselves about that. . .

"Now, we must rebuild our school system. There are only two
forces which can prevent this. The white people of North Carolina can prevent rebuilding of our schools if they are not courageous and wise and self-restrained. The Federal Courts can prevent
the rebuilding of our schools if they are not tolerant and patient
and conscious of the practicalities of the present situation.

"No Federal Court has said that there must be mixing of the
races—integration. No Federal Court has said that any child of
any race must be compelled to go to school with a child or
children of another race. This is of great importance. The precise
Supreme Court decision was that a law is invalid if it says that a
child can be excluded from a school solely because of race. But
no court has said that a child must go to a school with children
of another race. . .

"But an administrative body may well find, if it acts honestly and
in the light of local conditions, that under existing local conditions it may not be feasible or best for a particular child to go to
a particular school with children of another race. A color bar by
law is one thing. A factual local condition bar, even if color is
one of the causes of the condition, is a different thing. An understanding and tolerant Court may well recognize that difference. . .

"We believe that members of each race prefer to associate with
other members of their race and that they will do so naturally

unless they are prodded and inflamed and controlled by outside pressure.

"We think it is also true that children do best when in school with children of their own race. We think that in the course of time that will be plain to everyone. When the fires have subsided, when sanity returns, when the NAACP finds that it cannot use the Federal Courts as a club in a fight with the white people, and when the North Carolina Negro finds that his outside advisors are not his best or most reliable friends, then we can achieve the voluntary separation which our Governor and other State leaders have so wisely advocated.

"Until that time arrives we urge that memebers of both races act and speak with restraint and avoid an open break between the races which would make it impossible to approach the solution of our problem in a spirit of reason and cooperation. An attitude of tolerance and cooperation is responsible for the harmonious relations which the races have enjoyed in North Carolina for more than fifty years and accounts for the great progress which the Negro race has made in our State during that time. Given time, we hope that same attitude can be reestablished and will aid greatly in the solution of this, our greatest problem.

"Specifically, we recommend that all school units:

"1. Recognize that there is no law compelling the mixing of the races.

"2. Recognize that since the Supreme Court decision there can be no valid law compelling the separation of the races in public schools.

"3. Declare that initial assignments to schools will be made in accordance with what the assigning unit (or officer) considers to be for the best interest of the child assigned, including in its consideration, residence, school attended during the preceding year, availability of facilities, and all other local conditions bearing upon the welfare of the child and the prospective effectiveness of his school

"4. After initial assignments are made, permit transfers only upon application and hearing in due course and in accordance with the provisions of the 1955 assignment law.

"The schools of our State are so intimately related to the customs and feelings of the people of each community that their effective operation is impossible except in conformity with community attitudes.

"It may well be that before the people of North Carolina will give the necessary support to an honest trial of the assignment plan they will need to be assured of escape possibilities from intolerable situations—assured first that no child will be forced to attend a school with the children of another race in order to get an education and assured, second, that if a public school situation becomes intolerable to a community, the school or schools in that community may be closed."

Several aspects of this statement are worth comment. The first is that it is impossible not to feel the iron hand of determination beneath the silk glove of its repressed expression. Regardless of whether we agree or disagree with them these are the most responsible leaders of the State speaking and they leave no doubt that they are in earnest. Likewise anyone who has followed the results of recent elections will know that they speak for the overwhelming majority of the white people in counties which have large percentages of Negro population.

The second remarkable aspect of this report is its frank advocacy of compliance by the technique of evasion. It says plainly that although it is illegal to segregate on the basis of race, it is possible to accomplish much the same result by setting up other bases for separation. This enunciation of policy would seem to forecast a situation relative to segregation closely similar to the one which has evolved in the case of disfranchisement where the privilege to vote is extended on a selective basis when the community considers itself ready for such a move. In other words unlike the other six states, the statement does not recommend defiance of the law but accommodation to the law while maintaining the Southern customs to the maximum extent possible.

Again, the statement tacitly recognizes that the course recommended may result in some desegregation and differs again from the other six Deep South states in paying at least lip service to local determination of policy.

The most alarming feature of the recommendations (which has now been enacted into law) is the provision that if, under pressure from the federal courts, the mixing of pupils is decreed before the community is ready for it, the local authorities may close the public schools. This is, of course, legally possible since there is no federal compulsion to provide public education. As pointed out, however, this would be a backward step of catastrophic consequences not only for the Negroes, who are ill equipped to operate efficient private schools, but also for the poorer white families, who might find this too expensive. For all pupils it would mean the jeopardy of standards, deterioration of equipment, and demoralization of a teaching staff which is now trained, supervised, and protected by a uniform salary scale and retirement privileges.

This North Carolina statement has been reproduced at such length both because it is indicative of the depth and scope of the conservative attitude on desegregation and because it may typify the course which will eventually be taken by the other six Deep South states when they realize the utter futility of inflexible defiance of the Supreme Court. In short, it would appear that this is the situation which will prevail in the Deep South well into the 1960's, namely that the sentiment of the white community is such that desegregation in the schools will be held to a minimum and will come very gradually. On the other hand, as long as the segregated facilities are inferior there will be continued pressure and more legal action looking to the equalization of opportunity.

The report of the North Carolina Commission represents one attempt to outline a working arrangement under the ruling of the Court but others will disagree with their interpretation. In short nobody seems to know for sure just what the Delphic utterance of the Court on segregation means and many attempts at amateur interpretation have been made. What the Court said was that the job of desegregation should be undertaken with all deliberate speed and that the acceptable rate of progress was to be interpreted by the lower federal courts. The extremists on one side think it should be the speed of a greyhound, those on the other think it should be closer to that of a tortoise. If the courts rule in accordance with the social and economic variations within the South, "deliberate" will be interpreted differently in different situations. On the basis of the few cases which have been decided so far this would seem to be the attitude of the judges. Some cases in which the community involved appeared to be planning in good faith to comply eventually were decided in favor of the community. Others in which defiance and determination to make no move was apparent were decided against the community. It would therefore appear that unless the two races of the South can, themselves, work out reasonably satisfactory solutions in each community the people and the courts will be plagued by these suits for years to come.

It is well known that lawsuits are the surest way to inflame tempers and destroy friendships. It would, of course, be possible to delay the inevitable by waiting for legal compulsion in each county but this would prove costly and damaging to orderly progress. That is not a pleasant prospect. It would be far more advantageous in the long run for Southern communities to exhaust every effort to find a workable basis for cooperation in the harmonious development of the region.

CHAPTER 16

Racial Differences: Fact and Fancy

In the preceding chapters racial difference has been frequently cited both as one of the chief causes and one of the chief effects of prejudice, discrimination, and segregation. This is true whether the difference is real or fancied. A strong feeling of difference governs the conduct of one race to another. It must be taken into account to explain any aspect of race relations or to plan any constructive measure.

Some of the visible differences between the average Negro and the average white man are quite obvious. Some which were claimed by intelligent people in my young manhood were quite fantastic and fictional. They were on a par with the racial theory announced by the eloquent antebellum Negro evangelist, John Jasper, who charmed audiences of both races with such gems as: There are four great races of man, the Hottentots, the Huguenots, the Abyssinians and the Virginians.

Such naive beliefs are still encountered in isolated areas, some have been dispelled in the light of experience. One of these exploded myths was that the Negro lacked the native capacity for handling machinery. This was widely held despite the example of Benjamin Banneker, a pre-revolutionary freed Negro who was reputed to be one of New England's best early clockmakers and gained some reputation as a mathematician. It ignored the many skilled sawyers and cotton-gin operators of the slave plantations and it overlooked Jan E. Matzeliger, who in 1883 patented a machine for lasting shoes which laid the foundation for the present American shoe manufacturing processes.

But I can see how this belief could gain credence. My wife once undertook to train a woman fresh from the corn field to cook. (Incidentally she eventually turned out to be a good cook.) On her first experience with an electric waffle iron she was bemused by the question, "How do de fire get in?" and when she was offered a waffle to eat she said, "No thanks, but I would love to take one home for the children to play with".

In fact most of these myths of race difference had enough truth in them to make them plausible. For instance it was clearly a fact that in the early days of my generation the Negro death rate was about twice as high as the white rate, that the deaths of infants were tragically high, that the deaths from tuberculosis and pneumonia were especially prevalent. These made it possible to believe that the Negro was, by heredity, physically inferior to the white man in coping with modern civilization. No one then foresaw the astounding advances in public health and medicine which were about to emerge to demonstrate that, with education and intelligent control these conditions are remediable.

This question of racial difference became one of absorbing interest to social scientists in the 1930's. The University of Chicago began its intensive studies with that city as its laboratory. The University of North Carolina carried out extensive analysis of the Southern Region. The Laura Spelman Rockefeller Foundation subsidized numerous studies. The newly organized Social Science Research Council and the Population Association of America gave increasing attention to race and various government agencies added to the mountain of statistics and special reports. Sociologists, anthropologists, psychologists, historians, geographers, public health workers, social workers, and others looked at the phenomenon from different angles.

At last a body of authenticated facts was accumulating as a substitute for the opinions of the previous century. These researches were summarized as far as it was possible for one group of men to do so by Gunnar Myrdal's study undertaken under the auspices of the Carnegie Foundation just before World War II. Even so this summary required over 1,000 pages to present. Progress has been so great since then that this work is now, in certain respects, out of date. In fact the tempo of racial progress has been so speeded up that conclusions must be continually revised to keep up with changing trends.

Race relations are dynamic and change as economic and social institutions change. This, in itself, is a fact which is not sufficiently taken into account by those who cling to beliefs about race difference based on stereotypes inherited from ancestral tradition.

Unfortunately few scientific investigators present their findings in such a form as to be readily digested by the man in the street. They must be translated into textbooks and presented to students who, in their turn, must age a little more before their views are taken seriously; or they must find their way piecemeal into pamphlets, speeches, or sermons prepared for popular consumption. Then the new fact must fight it out with previous misconceptions. This lag between the discovery of facts and their general acceptance is, in a way, insurance against the spread of half truths before they are tested. On the other hand this lag explains, to some extent, the persistence in some segments of the population of horse and buggy ideas in a jet age.

The scientific studies explored many types of difference—historical, physical, mental, economic, and social. There is space here to mention only some of the most significant findings.

Historically we learn that the colored Americans who are called Negroes are not, properly speaking, a race. Those who go to the Bible for racial origins pick Ham, the son of Noah, as the ancestor of Negroes. They overlook the fact that Ham and his brothers had one father and that in the ages since Ham and his wife came out of the ark and presumably moved to the tropics and turned black, their descendants have visited among and been visited by many peoples. Africans who were brought to this country were a varied group—a mixture of different Negro stocks with some Arabic infusion. Furthermore, they no sooner arrived on these shores than infusions of Indian and white blood began and continued for over a century, with the result that it is impossible to find large groups that would be expected to have "typically Negro" traits except in a few isolated areas.

As true of all mixed peoples, it was found that the measurement of physical traits and native intelligence disclosed as wide a range of variation within the so-called Negro group as within the white. Some differences in group averages were found but not enough to affect materially the ability of the average individual to function efficiently as a member of modern society. Around these averages there was a broad distribution resulting in a considerable overlap between the individuals of the white and Negro groups which were compared. Even in such a trait as skin color the lighter "Negro" individuals are not so dark as the more swarthy persons of white parentage. Efforts to compare groups in such complex traits as musical ability, language facility or mathematical aptitude showed even more overlap. Small wonder then that the careful scientist is hesitant to generalize as to "Negro" traits.

Aside from skin color, hair texture, and facial traits—all superficial—the differences most often noted are those of attitude and behavior. Tendencies to exhibit higher disease rates, higher crime rates, less thrift, and slower learning have been emphasized

as inherited traits when, as a matter of fact, the voluminous research on the subject demonstrated that these characteristics cannot be inherited but arise from differences in social tradition and
democratic opportunity, and, that as the level of education rises,
and home life and economic status improve, these differences
become less pronounced.

In short there is no evidence that the Negro is an inferior
human being. On the other hand, there is overwhelming evidence
that, as a group, he is still sharply differentiated from white
Americans by the long-standing, systematic denial of equal opportunity to share in the good things of democracy. The most
basic opportunities which are denied to Negroes but which or-
dinary Americans receive as a matter of course are the denial of
the vote, the denial of equal job opportunities, and the denial
of equal educational opportunities.

As we saw in Chapter 14, there have been times when the Negro
exercised his right to vote with a minimum of interference. During the first half of this century, however, in most of the South,
he has been effectively and almost totally deprived of political
power. For two generations he has had no voice in the formulation of policy or the choice of the elected administrators of policy.
Politically the Negro has taken just what the white man was willing to give him and nothing more. The white man, whose ancestors bled to escape taxation without representation, has not
hesitated to tax the property, the income, and the retail purchases
of the colored man without allowing him the slightest voice in
determining the benefits which he received for his money.

The denial of this right has made the Negro a fatalist, per-
petuating his psychology of dependence on the white man. Although it is possible that without the vote the Negro could be
given equality before the law and an equal share of public benefits, he still would receive these as a gift, not something which he
secured by his own efforts. Nor could he ever be sure that they
would not be taken away on the whim of the donor.

The denial of equal job opportunities has come about through
the separation of the economy into compartments, one labeled
Negro jobs, the other white jobs, and by the traditionally lower
wage for Negro jobs. These distinctions have been relatively less
rigid in times of labor shortage than in times when labor was
plentiful. But the pattern has been sufficiently rigid to place the
Negro worker at the bottom of the economic ladder and to herd

him into the least desirable slum and near-slum living quarters.

His incentive to give a full day's work for a full day's pay has been deadened by the knowledge that full productive effort will not be rewarded by something better. His low income has restricted his choice of living quarters to slum and near slum areas and prejudice has kept him there, branding him with the reputation for poor health and crime which are the badges of slum dwellers the world over.

The denial of educational opportunity is linked both with the denial of the political power to secure larger appropriations and the low family income which force him to leave school and go to work earlier. Limitations of job opportunities also rob many of the incentive to learn. Negroes have for so long heard white men claim that they are incapable of learning that it would be remarkable if many could escape the feeling that perhaps that is true. He has it so constantly dinned into his ears that he is disadvantaged that he gets an inferiority complex and develops self-pity. The feeling of difference colors his whole personality making him in some respects his own worst enemy by imposing the disheartening handicap of having to rise above himself.

When white men point the finger at the Negro as a race and say "We no not like you because you are so different," they are, in part, criticising the product of their own handiwork and castigating the Negro for failure to attain a stature which he has been denied the opportunity to attain. To "keep the Negro in his place" simply means keep him within the web of discrimination woven around him.

It would be a mistake to leave the impression that all Negroes have felt the impact of these denials equally. The chance to share in the democratic process has, with the exception of economic opportunity, been fairly equal in Northern communities, somewhat less so in Border States, and least in the Deep South—and even there advantages have been greater in the city than on the farm. For this reason the rapid shift of the population to the cities and to the North, has, in itself, accelerated progress and thereby promoted more conformity with American standards. There are, however, stagnant pools of population into which progress has not flowed strongly, where opportunity is still limited, and where, consequently, there are wide differences in the attitude and behavior of the races. These differences have been widened by a selective migration which drains out the ambitious and energetic Negroes who seek greater opportunity, leaving behind the improvident and listless to typify the whole race in the eyes of their neighbors. The Negroes who remain in the disadvantaged areas of the Black Belts differ about as much from the second generation Northern Negro as they do from white people.

It would also be a mistake to leave the impression that these cultural differences are fixed and stationary. To the extent that they are determined by denial of opportunity, they are remediable by access to opportunity. The progress of the Negro in most sections of the Nation has been nothing short of phenomenal since World War II and it will be extremely difficult to reverse this current which runs so strongly. Although it will require at least a generation for the full effects of more equal advantage to become fully apparent, already even the superficial observer can note the emergence of a New Negro. In the preceding chapters there is ample encouragement in the progress recorded in politics, economics, and education.

There are also other fields which have not been dwelt on at length in which encouraging progress has been made. There are: health, family stability, and acceptance by the general public of the Negro as a competitive athlete and artist. It was the fleet-footedness of Jesse Owens at the Berlin Olympic Games that compelled that arch-racist Hitler to award the palm of the victor to a colored man. It was the golden voice of Marian Anderson echoed from the portico of Lincoln Memorial which changed the ban of the Daughters of the American Revolution against the use of their national auditorium by Negroes. It was the magnificent performances of the Negro casts of Green Pastures and Porgy and Bess which accustomed white audiences to Negro actors in other than comedy roles.

The measure of progress made to date marks the distance still to go before the American Negro is just another American. It reemphasizes the responsibilities of Negro leaders to do their share in eliminating racial difference. Now that the courts have decided with the Negro intelligentsia that they should not be locked in by the walls of segregation with their less advantaged brothers, or locked out of the most modern facilities, they can, in time, devote less attention to demands and litigation and more to promoting the philosophy of learning and earning. They can give thought to sharing some of their advantages with the less fortunate.

After all, it is more important to secure a good education than to be educated in the same room as white children. A good education cannot be given to any group simply by the provision of facilities and teachers. It requires effort on the part of parents and children and a determination to make the most of improved schools.

It is more important to get and hold a good job than it is to work side by side with a white man. Removal of job prejudice may help one to get a good job but only by the demonstration of skill and acceptable work habits can one hold the job in competition with other workers. Above all it is important to vote but it is more important to vote on the issues rather than as a member of a race. At present Negro politics is somewhat like the baseball loyalties of the maid of a friend of mine; when he was listening to the all-star game, she came in frequently—not to ask the score but to see if a colored man made a hit.

It is more important that the masses of underpriviledged children have decent recreation facilities than that a few who want to keep up with the Joneses be allowed to play golf with the white people. Segregation is only a symbol of more basic denials, a device by which the denials are enforced. The Negro feels, probably correctly, that if this stigma of difference is removed, the discrimination which is at the root of difference will disappear sooner. Undoubtedly its removal would go far in eliminating the Negro's own feeling of inferiority.

The white men of America, in larger and larger numbers, are welcoming the extension of the opportunities which close the gap between the races made by discrimination in the past for this is the only way in which the nation can make full use of its human resources. It is highly doubtful that discrimination would have ever been so severe had there been fuller recognition of the extent that the denial of equal opportunity handicapped the South. The retarded training of the Negro has saddled the South with an archaic system of agriculture and, until recently, discouraged the development of industry. As long as the Negro remained half educated he was a perpetuator of slums and inefficiency. Low wages sapped the desire to do good work.

The apologists for racial discrimination often use race differences as their excuse. They should be constantly reminded, however, that the area of similarity among human beings is far broader than the area of difference. We should also keep in mind that the differences between individuals are one of the pleasant things of life and that progress arises from variety and not from uniformity. The effort to minimize difference should therefore be directed toward those variations which are created by unequal opportunity rather than the differences of aptitude and personality.

In a society founded on rugged individualism there will always be differences but more and more the undesirable differences will be recognized as springing from denial of an equal share in the benefits of democracy rather than from different racial inheritance. More Americans need to develop a broad tolerance of difference that will separate fact from fantasy and emphasize the traits which promote cooperation rather than those which lead to dissention.

CHAPTER 17

The Way to Harmony

The habit of working together on a personal basis has always been widespread in the South. The necessity to harmonize the daily chores of making a living permeates the whole economic and social system. Due to the weaker position of the Negro, however, the proposed terms of cooperation were often arbitrary and unacceptable to him. They had much of the flavor of the type of labor relations advocated by one of the industrialists of the 1890's who said that he wanted cooperation and that it meant "Do what I say and do it damn quick."

Much more genuine mutual assistance was characteristic of the program of the Southern Education Board and of the educational foundations. It had been popularized at least in part by the eloquent good will tours so frequently made by Booker T. Washington. As a matter of fact, cooperative relationships have always far outnumbered those involving conflict, but unfortunately the latter have attracted the most publicity, especially outside the South.

There was then, in 1920, a foundation for the organization of the Commission on Interracial Cooperation in the South. This movement, active into the 1940's, was designed to strengthen and harness the existing spirit of cooperation, give it respectability, and make it an effective instrument for harmonious progress.

We have described in Chapter IV its accomplishments, along with other organizations, in the campaign to discredit violence as a method of settling racial differences. I worked with this organization actively for six years in the 1920's, and I believe that, while the campaign against violence was the most spectacular part of its program, that was negative and defensive. Its more basic objectives were to spread the philosophy of cooperation between the leaders of the races on the basis of frankness, man to man; to secure the participation of Negroes as full participants in constructive programs; and to create a climate of public opinion favorable to the operation of other organizations concerned with progress in the South.

Although, the foundation and precedent for cooperation existed, formal organization and a program and machinery for carrying it to the grass roots were lacking. This was supplied by state and county committees. County committees were organized in over eight hundred counties. By no means were all of these county committees active in the sense of meeting regularly but they were there on call in case of need and to serve as a symbol of the cooperative ideal. In a sense they accomplished something by just being in existence.

The first job was to get acquainted. On the state level this was not too difficult because men of statewide prominence in both races knew a little about one another. Strangely enough it was in the smaller places where everybody is supposed to know everybody else that contacts between the leaders of the races had been least. Contacts on the plantation had been between the white landlords and ignorant croppers and in the towns between the white employers and Negro domestic servants or unskilled laborers. Thus, while some Negroes might know one or two prominent white people, the white leaders who controlled the community were hardly conscious of the prominent Negroes and certainly not fully aware of their feelings and ambitions. The Negro preachers, teachers, business men and doctors were obscured by the color line. Often in the early days of the movement you could hear the expression, "I did not know that such people existed".

Who were these people who were getting together for the first time? Aside from being community leaders what were their qualifications? I would say that their outstanding characteristic was courage. We must keep in mind that this venture was made in the heyday of the Ku Klux when it was impossible in many communities to be elected or appointed to even a minor office without the endorsement of the Klan. The white leaders, therefore, had to be secure enough in their position or serene enough in their belief to ignore the scurrilous attacks based on the appeal to prejudice. Negro leaders had to be courageous for another reason. They had to step cautiously to avoid offending the white people on the one hand or losing their own following through overcaution on the other. Some of the wisdom and technique of the Southern Negro leaders is illustrated in quotations which Ralph Bunche picked up in his travels through the region.

"Don't emphasize the Negro's right—don't *press* for anything— make him [the white man] feel he's a big man, get to other white men to make him want to avoid seeming small, and you

can make him jump through the barrel. You can make him a
friend or a rattlesnake, depending on your approach."

Or, "I am a respectable citizen, but when I try to get my rights
I do so in a way that will not be obnoxious, and not in a radical
way. I don't believe in radicalism. We *ask* for things, but never
demand. When I am in Rome, I burn Roman candles . . . but I
don't 'Uncle Tom.' "

Again, "If a Negro goes so far as to make an enemy of the
white man who has the power he is foolish. You can't hit a man
in the mouth and expect him to loan you money. . . . A man
wouldn't be head of a big concern if he wasn't a smart man, and
a smart man will always react to facts. My approach is to the
fellow on top because he is going to have to take care of me and I
must work for him—he has the stick."

In truth nothing but altruism could then, or now, induce comfortable Southern people of either race to advocate moderation.
They cannot expect to be popular or gain any personal advantage.
The rabid race haters castigate them for going too far, and from
their pleasant ivory towers in the North, the starry-eyed professional sympathizers sneer at them for not going far enough. I am
convinced, however, that it was a social miracle that, in the
vexed crisis of the 1920's, anything at all was accomplished.

The white leaders were not only surprised to discover such intelligent Negro neighbors but some were surprised to discover
likeminded men of their own race. There are, and always have
been, many men in the South who are tolerant and fair-minded.
Every community has some. They are not ordinarily articulate on
race matters. They don't spout their views from the housetops and
thus are often not aware of the views of their own friends. Such
men discovered in the interracial organization the moral support
of other leaders and a channel for expressing themselves.

They had to overcome old habits of association. I remember
one county meeting where a new Negro school was under discussion. One of the white members, trying to be liberal but not
realizing the implications of his remark to the Negroes said: "Sure
I believe in training; my old dog Bose is the best trained pointer
in the county". Bose who was present thumped his tail on the
floor in appreciation but the Negroes did not appreciate the
analogy. Usually, however, both groups went to great lengths to
exercise courtesy and tact and make a genuine effort to explore
each other's mind without reservations.

Mutual acquaintance came from meeting together, mutual confidence they had, and the third requisite of cooperation, mutual respect, came from working together. Committees would sometimes start out by holding philosophical discussions on race relations and brotherhood. But unless they could progress beyond the theoretical stage they did not hold together long because busy men have no time for long dissertations on social philosophy. The successful committees were those whose members learned to cooperate by cooperating. The Negroes would make some concrete request such as for assistance in securing a new school, less brutality on the part of the police, improvement in sanitation, or some provision for public recreation. At one meeting which I attended the Negro spokesman made his plea for street improvement by saying, "Friends, we certainly would like a smoother street on the two blocks from the main street to our cemetery. That stretch is so rough now that every time we have a funeral the corpse almost jolts out of the hearse."

The requests were so reasonable and so like the aims of the white community that they were usually taken up with enthusiasm and worked out mutually.

Sometimes the request for cooperation went in the other direction. The white members would ask the Negroes to solicit support for a clean-up drive, a community chest campaign or other project of common concern. These were equally successful and a few successes instilled in the committess a real pride in working together.

I know that these were not earth-shaking accomplishments. Many of them fell into the category of removing the gravel from the shoe of the Negro who wished to progress. On the other hand the lesson of cooperation was learned and the improvement of the racial climate was real.

The Interracial Commission did not conceive its mission to be solving the race problem by grandiose and sensational moves but believed that the so-called race problem was the accumulation of a large number of problems growing out of day-to-day relationships which, if not handled with sympathy and understanding, mounted up to an accumulation of misunderstanding, irritation, and even bitterness.

The Interracial Commission was able to secure the support of many of the most influential leaders of Southern public opinion including prominent editors, educators, and ministers. Few business men or politicians, however, were willing to risk their popularity. They were doubly fortunate to have, all through the early years, the guiding hand of W. W. Alexander, a man trained as a minister, whose close touch with the problems of the South and whose broad tolerance and patience made him an inspiration to the members.

The state and South-wide committees set themselves to general tasks of influencing public opinion but with occassional pressure on administrators in connection with key decisions.

Before that period little news about Negroes appeared in the daily press unless it related to crime. When the name of a Negro who had been arrested was printed, the paper was careful to label him as a Negro, which seemed about as logical to the law-abiding Negroes as it would have been to mention the hair color of every redheaded person who became entangled with the law. Through the inclusion of as many editors as possible on the committees, through addresses before conventions of editors and through issuing a series of news releases which reported creditable actions of Negroes, the Commission gradually changed the policy of a substantial segment of the Southern daily press, increasing the space given to favorable news and playing down news which could cause friction.

Church groups had always been the most tolerant and readily joined in the fight for justice with conspicuous success.

College faculties and students were increasingly open-minded on race questions but had little ammunition in the way of systematically complied facts. In a survey of Southern colleges which I made for the Commission, only one or two were discovered which gave as much as a three months' course on race. A few more included some lectures on race in more general sociological courses. This interest was stimulated and broadened by sending informed lecturers to colleges wherever they were invited.

There was no comprehensive textbook which could be used by those study groups so I was assigned the job of writing one. In rereading it I am impressed by the fact that it was not a very good job and would, in comparison to present day texts, be considered wholly inadequate. I can only plead immaturity and lack of systematically developed facts as reasons for its shortcoming. Nevertheless, it was soon adopted as the basis for courses in race relations in some sixty Southern colleges.

Up to that time analytical literature on race was not too voluminous. Some community surveys gave firsthand descriptions of local situations. A few works had appeared on the plantation system and on educational conditions and a considerable number of essays on the philosophy of race were in print. What I did was try to put these together.

It was not until the late 1920's that extensive, systematic, factual books became common. Since then hundreds of thousands of pages of factual reports, surveys, monographs, and propaganda about the Negro have been published. It is almost beyond the power of human eyesight to read it all. The production of more objectively determined facts soon made it possible to produce more comprehensive and systematic texts for study groups.

Literally hundreds of thousands of students in both Northern and Southern colleges have been exposed to the hard facts of race relations in the past thirty years. Their minds have been disabused in varying degrees of the folk myths about race. They know that the Negro is not inferior—different to some extent but not fundamentally. They know that violence, discrimination, and intolerance have no moral sanction and accomplish nothing. They know that social disorganization indexed by high rates of illegitimacy, crime, and disease do not come from a racial inheritance but from environment and lack of opportunity. Probably the most fundamental change in thinking which came from learning was the doubt cast on the often repeated beliefs that "the Southerner is the only one who really knows the Negro" and that "Our Negroes are satisfied with conditions unless they are stirred up by outside agitators." The people with facts were also less susceptible to the idiocy of rumor and less credulous of the assertion of the demagog. Unfortunately most of them were below thirty-five years of age in 1955 and their generation was not yet fully in control of Southern policy. They must work things out with a majority of less instructed leaders who still cling dogmatically to old conceptions of race.

Although I naturally favor free speech I sometimes believe we would get along better if everybody over thirty-five, myself included, could be prohibited from discussing race especially when running for political office. The younger people are the ones who will have to work things out during the last half of the twentieth century.

In addition to the colleges the YM and YWCA's provided systematic study groups. From the National Headquarters John Mott was a staunch advocate of the study of race relations and cooperation in developing Negro YMCA's. In the Southern region the writings and organizing ability of W. D. Weatherford were influential.

Summer student conferences of the YMCA included, as a regular part of their program, lectures and discussion of race. It was sometimes difficult to keep these students, in their youthful enthusiasm, from violating the conventions to the extent of alienating their elders. An incident in point came at the conference of Arkansas, Oklahoma, and Texas students at Hollister, Missouri, when Texas, with its usual enthusiasm was going all out for Ku Kluxery. Major Moton, the Negro principal of Tuskegee, came to lecture. As usual his meals were served at the leader's table but his first address met such enthusiasm that one of the Texas boys came over and invited him to eat at the Texas table. I was seated next to the Major and, if it can be said the black man can blush, he did. He managed to stammer some polite but convincing refusal and told me the next morning that he had imagined that he could hear the Ku Klux riding up and down in front of the camp all night.

After the organization period the Commission was able to systematize this work of supplying lecturers to the point that speakers could be secured in response to almost every important request. One of the most impressive and effective exhibits used was George Washington Carver who, as a sickly slave child, had been discarded by slave raiders and left to die by the roadside. He was rescued and nursed to health by a white man and lived to work his way through Iowa State College. Carver's profound impression on Southern audiences came, not as the result of his oratory, but of his accomplishments and his personality. What he had been able to do with the native clay, peanuts and sweet potatoes was marvelous, but his devout, earnest, and modest bearing was even more impressive. He was humble, not in the sense of kowtowing to the white men, but in a genuine awe before the great forces of nature. I asked him once whether he classified himself as an agricultural scientist, a botanist, or a chemist. His reply was, "Most of the things that I do are just cookery. These are not my products, God put them here and I found them." Such mysticism did not appeal to the professional chemists with fancy degrees and highbrow writings. They were inclined to take issue with such modest simplicity, and take exception to such disregard of the academic trappings.

I have in my home a valued memento of the versatility and warm spirit of Carver. Together we had observed the varied clays on the banks of a creek near Tuskegee and when I married he went to the creek, dug out an assortment of clays, and painted a pastel of the scene for my wedding present. He was also a passable artist and the clay colors in the picture are unchanged after thirty years.

Of course Major Moton, Principal of Tuskegee, was another Negro called on to speak on many occasions. He was over six feet tall, very black, and one whose persuasive tongue and powerful voice could always sway audiences. There was also Isaac Fisher, of Fisk University. The brilliance of his style was evidenced by an award won in open competion for an article on "What I Know about Rum". From his description one could literally see and smell the whole malodorous process.

Other efforts to acquaint the South with the rich contributions of the Negro race involved seeking audiences for singers. One such venture was arranging a concert for Roland Hayes in the Atlanta public auditorium. This was a packed-house performance and a smashing success. We also found openings for school quartets and choruses.

It occurred to me in this connection to explore the new medium of radio, which was then a lusty infant not far away from the crystal set—earphone stage. I approached station WSB, of the Atlanta Journal, with the idea of scheduling the Tuskegee quartette. That was fine. There was no hesitation. They just hadn't thought of it before. It was before the days of fan mail but there were indications of a cordial reception of the program. The appearances of Negroes on radio and television are now so commonplace that their absence from the public eye in the South at such a recent period is hardly credible.

Committees were also encouraged to secure more Negro participation in civic affairs. Community chests were particularly responsive. No difficulty was encountered in including Negro YMCA's, YWCA's, clinics, orphanages, and Urban League chapters in the appeal for funds and certainly none in the organization of the campaign to reach Negro donors.

When the community chest was organized in Atlanta it was my pleasure to serve as liason between the Negro committee and the main committee. (It was not until later that Negroes were included on the main committee). It was a great joy to attend the meetings at which the Negroes reported on the progress of their drives. With the enthusiasm of a boy for a new bicycle, they always subscribed more than they could eventually pay but a substantial amount was actually contributed and the lapses were forgiven on the grounds of overzeal for well-doing. The thing which inspired such overpowering interest among the Negroes in the project was not only the worthwhileness of the chest program to their people but the fact that they were being consulted and asked to participate on an equal footing with the other community leaders.

The Interracial Commission continued in a formal way into the 1940's. Recent trends have made it less necessary to have so widespread an organization. There has been a steadily rising number of programs for community improvement which function interracially as a matter of course. Community business is more highly organized in the South than it was before the depression. Now soil conservation districts, county agricultural programs, health programs, and public welfare activities have the habit of more or less automatically seeking Negro cooperation. The good seed has sprouted.

But the idea of a common forum for racial discussion is still alive. While I was drafting these pages one of the press services carried the report of the formation of such a committee by the mayor of Mobile, Alabama. During the controversy over the desegregation of schools in Charlottesville, Virginia, an interracial committee was formed in that city also to work for compliance with the decision of the court. These are only two examples of the numerous cooperative groups scattered through the South. Several Southern Governors have proposed that state committees be set up by legislative action and President Eisenhower proposed similar national action by the Congress. It is not necessary, and probably not desirable, that a state or national executive secure legislative approval. One of the chief strengths of the Interracial Commission was that it was not hampered by politics. At most what such a body needs from the executive is his official blessing.

The original Interracial Commission undoubtedly made mistakes. One which is apparent in retrospect was its almost entire dependence on foundation grants for financial support. A greater effort to build indigenous financing would have been more effective, but Southern moderates are not usually from the monied class. A second criticism which was lodged against the movement,

with considerable justification, was that it was not bold enough,
that it was too prone to implant the philosophy of cooperation
without pushing for more spectacular action. In any case this is a
matter of judgement. The conscientious conviction of the members was that its modest gains would have been endangered by
trying to push ahead too rapidly in the atmosphere of hostility
which was encountered from formidable powers at that time.

A substantial part of the Southern support of the Commission
was given because its philosophy was to adhere tacitly to the
"separate but equal" objective in race relations. In the 1940's however, the Southern Negro leaders began to press vigorously for a
platform which would unequivocally oppose forced segregation.
Accordingly the Southern Regional Council, the organization suc-
cessor to the Commission on Interracial Cooperation, adopted a
forthright stand on this principle.

In taking this stand it was feared that the council would lose
a substantial number of its former Southern white members. This
was a pessimistic forecast. As it turned out a surprising number
stuck with the new program and this number will certainly increase as time passes.

The spirit of cooperation has always been stronger among the
Southern clergy than in other groups. The controversy over segregation, however, has divided the churches also. They too are having to do some soul searching.

My television screen recently brought me the revolting spectacle
of a minister in Montgomery, Alabama, cloaked in Ku Klux regalia, using his "spiritual" influence to rouse the rabble to race
hatred. The rector of famous old St. Michael's Church in Charleston, South Carolina, was forced to resign because he would not
endorse the action of his vestrymen in passing a resolution which
barred Negroes from receiving communion. The Catholic Church
in Louisiana has been split because the Archbishop threatened to
excommunicate any member who agitated for segregation. Some
of his flock refer to him profanely and say they will be excom-
municated before they send their children to mixed schools. If
the Archbishop cannot sway his members, what chance has the
Supreme Court? The Methodist and Baptist denominations, to
which the majority of Southerners belong, are having great difficulty in formulating a policy relating to the Negro congregations
affiliated with them.

In general, the ranks of the clergy divide like the laymen on the basis of age. The younger, more recent graduates of the theological seminaries, are less swayed by tradition, more willing to preach cooperation and tolerance, and more inclined to emphasize the brotherhood of man as the key to Christain conduct and the way to peace on earth.

But the South can change and has changed. It is not generally realized that the South, more than any other section of the nation, has been subjected to sudden and violent redirections of its policy. First the long-established institution of slavery which had had the sanction of the church, the political leadership, the courts and, for some decades, most of the rest of the nation, was swept away. After several decades of uneasy balance, the pendulum was swung in the other direction by the race baiters and sixty years of disfranchisement and segregation crystallized new customs. In the mid-1950's the courts and apparently the majority sentiment of other regions called for another reversal of policy. The South can adjust to this new situation also if its leaders approach the task with honesty and courage and in the spirit of cooperation rather than in the bitterness of controversy. But it will take time.

When one of these recurring controversies has reached the boiling point three broad groups have always emerged: (1) The protesters who include the impatient Negro leaders who are not administrators but who expect the administrators to perform miracles yesterday; these have as their allies the professional sympathizers. (2) The conservatives, including Southerners who want no change and race hating fanatics who think that the Negro should have no consideration. (3) Between these two are the moderates of both races who are confronted with the practical difficulty of preventing either of the extremist groups from scaling the heights of assdom and of devising workable solutions for the ever present problems of bi-racial living.

In the heat of controversy the extreme factions put aside conciliation, placing the desire to win an argument ahead of potential reaction. The idealists are often extremely bitter and intemperate in their attacks on the South. Human nature being what it is, the counteraction of the extremist Southern groups is equally as violent and intemperate often taking the form of retaliatory action against the Southern Negro who is caught between the combatants. In their reaction against the pressure to desegregate schools and the accompaning castigation of the South, the Southern stand-pat groups have lashed out with many irrational reprisals. I was in Alabama at the time of Autherine Lucy's unsuccessful attempt to attend the university and observed that the legislature, then in session, had before it no less than 21 retaliatory bills—some silly, some serious. A number of Southern States have passed reprisal measures aimed at the National Association for the Advancement of Colored People which skate perilously close to the denial of the freedom of association and the freedom of speech. Mixed athletic competition was one field which the original framers of the Jim Crow laws overlooked but in 1956 the Louisiana Legislature hastily corrected this by jamming through a ban against bi-racial athletic contests. The result of this policy, if adhered to, will reduce the Sugar Bowl games which were rapidly becoming an outstanding athletic event and incidentally bringing thousands of tourist dollars into the state, to a local contest between Southern teams of no national significance. Again we have already noted that the united drive of the AFL-CIO to organize the South has been measurably set back by the effort to inject segregation as an issue. One proposal was to organize splinter all-white unions whose purpose would be to preserve segregation rather than promote the interests of all labor.

Both the extreme factions work largely through organizations which are dependent on strong emotional appeals to win votes or recruit members. They often give the impression that as long as they can stir up their constituents they are careless as to what incidental damage they may do.

The Southern inflammatory organizations have borne different names at different times: The Ku Klux, the Knights of the Camelia, the Organization for the Preservation of States' Rights, the White Citizens Councils, etc. But whatever the name, the purpose and method of operation have always been the same—to preserve the status quo, even if it impedes progress, and to do this by inflammatory appeals to fear and hatred of the Negro. No matter how law abiding their initial pronouncements sound, they often wind up by stirring up raw violence and defiance of the law.

On the other hand, while there have been other temporary protest organizations, the chief champion of the cause of the Negro has been the National Association for the Advancement of Colored People. This organization has needled the South so continuously and, on occassion, so successfully that it irritates the stand-pat Southerner like a cockleburr under a dog's tail. In contrast to the methods of the race-baiting organizations, the NAACP has always endeavored to work through the courts and the established channels for molding public opinion. It has been in existence for fifty years gaining in membership and influence and will, without doubt, be in business as long as the Negro feels himself so disadvantaged that he needs a powerful advocate.

When the tempest gets to such a violent stage that the extremist organizations attack each other intemperately, one is tempted to shout: "A plague on both your houses". But such extremes are necessary evils in the operation of the democratic process. If it were not for the protesters the conservatives would move too slowly and if it were not for the conservatives the protesters would make cooperation impossible by going to impractical extremes. Pulling and hauling in both directions are necessary to keep the moderates moving steadily up the middle of the road to progress. When the battle is at its height, however, the voices of the extremists all but drown out the voices of the moderates and the news agencies aid in their subordination by playing up the sensational, extreme acts and statements and ignoring prosaic, steady improvements. The moderates, not being able to swim against the tide of prejudice, go into temporary eclipse to wait for tempers to cool off, knowing all too well that when some compromise with which nobody is fully satisfied is agreed upon, it will be their job to work out the practical ways and means to restore cooperation and to strive for justice in the administrative machinery for making the new arrangement work.

Recurring tempests there will be, but each one will diminish in intensity. The areas with Negro majorities where cooperation is most difficult are steadily decreasing in number. The South is becoming more cosmopolitan. The widespread use of modern means of rapid transmission of news will promote the settlement of disputes on the basis of fact rather than fantasy even though the newsman's love for the sensational sometimes adds fuel to the fire of controversy. The national news services sent more reporters into the South to cover the desegregation controversy than were needed to cover a major war. I have read column after column of their dispatches and had I not known the South better I might have believed that a major war was about to start. But their reporting has stimulated more discussion of the issues of race relations than anything else could have done and that too is a necessary ingredient of democratic progress.

In my fifty years of close observation I have seen progress on the march. My reason for wanting to put these ideas on paper was to trace the footsteps of this encouraging advance. The rise in the status of the Negro in the past fifteen years has been truly remarkable and is not fully realized even by those who have lived close to it. Much of it has been brought about by the quiet, unspectacular cooperation of men of good will.

It is true that this progress has, in part, been attributable to population shifts to the cities and to the abounding prosperity of the national economy, but there has also been some closing of the gap between the status of the races, increase in tolerance, and a growth of acceptance of Negro progress as a matter of just deserts.

Except in the minds of the extremely prejudiced, there is now substantial agreement that the democratic ideal demands for every race full political participation, equal justice before the law, equal economic opportunity, and free access to the best public institutions. The differences which still divide public opinion and impede cooperation largely concern the practical questions of timing and methods rather than the ideal goal to be reached. This does not mean that the road ahead will not be rough at times nor that democracy will work without our best efforts to make it work.

At no time in the past fifty years has it been more imperative for men who believe firmly in cooperation to take the control of race relations out of the hands of the extremists and fire-eaters and shape the institutions of America to serve the true interests of both races, which are fundamentally the same.

National and state leadership can play their part by promoting needed legislation and creating a healthy public opinion but the major effort must be made in the local communities. Successful cooperation requires the continuing diligence of community leaders in securing the facts to ensure fair play, in creating a healthy public opinion, and in keeping the wheels of progress turning. Each community needs to know in detail what the real ambitions and grievances of its colored citizens are.

Fortunately there is a great and growing body of moderate community leaders, business and professional men, administrators, teachers, and preachers whose interest is not promoted by fanning race hatred but who are concerned with the orderly and successful transaction of the day-to-day business of the community. They hold the key to voluntary cooperation. It should be repeated that this task of moderate community leadership is primarily the job of the younger leaders. They are less bound by tradition and more tolerant; especially they are the ones who will have to live with the problem longest.

But community leaders cannot swing the job by themselves. Ultimately the success of cooperative community action must rest on the foundation of the spirit of mutual aid of the man in the street. The problems are too pressing in importance to American democracy for any one to be able to shirk his individual responsibility and leave the task to another. What each American needs is a code of conduct which enables him to look the members of any race in the eye and say: "I begrudge you no progress. I have not done and shall not do you harm."

If this Utopia could be approximated, organizations which thrive on race hatred could not take root. Protest organizations would have nothing to protest. Cooperative organizations would be unnecessary, because the pervasive spirit of cooperation would adjust race relations through the normal activities of the community and the state. But this ideal state cannot be approached until there is a more universal respect for facts rather than fantasy about race, a more widespread application of the golden rule, and a firmer faith in and support of the untrammeled operation of the democratic process.

Index

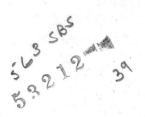